BEYOND THE
KAMA SUTRA

hamlyn

BEYOND THE
KAMA SUTRA

Eleanor McKenzie

First published in Great Britain in 2003 by
Hamlyn, a division of Octopus Publishing Group Ltd
2–4 Heron Quays, London E14 4JP

Copyright © Octopus Publishing Group Ltd 2003

ISBN 0 600 60741 0

A CIP catalogue record for this book is available from
the British Library

Printed and bound in China

10 9 8 7 6 5 4 3 2 1

CONTENTS

INTRODUCTION

Sex is the most profoundly intimate and creative way humans have of expressing themselves as they truly are. It is more profound than music, art or literature, and at the same time it is the impulse that fuels their creation. Sex is the heart of our humanity, and at its deepest level of expression, sex is not an accessory of love, but is love itself.

Most importantly, sex is a gift to be enjoyed by all of us, not just a few. Like most gifts, it needs constant practice to develop and thrive. Sex needs to be worked at, played with, talked, thought and read about. Sex is play and pleasure. It is also an act of devotion. As Havelock Ellis, the writer and early explorer of sexuality, said in *Studies in the Psychology of Sex* (1897–1910), '*Sex lies at the root of life, and we can never learn reverence for life until we learn reverence for sex.*'

ALL THE PLEASURES OF THE EAST

In the West we have no tradition of texts to guide us through what should be a lifetime of sexual adventure and exploration in which we discover ourselves as well as others. It is always easier to make a journey with a map. Some of the best maps available for our quest are ancient Eastern texts.

This book draws on all the major Eastern writings: the *Kama Sutra* and *Ananga Ranga*, the *Tao of Loving* and *The Perfumed Garden*. It also touches on the ideas found in the Tantric tradition and in the Japanese art of the geisha. Its aim is to illustrate and explain a range of sexual practices found in these texts and traditions from which you can pick and choose according to your taste.

It goes beyond the *Kama Sutra* because it goes beyond the confines of all the texts and blends their sexual practices into a contemporary exploration. It sets sexual practice in a modern context while also showing that when it comes to sex there is very little new under the sun – not even sex toys, which are as ancient as Mesopotamia.

CREATE YOUR OWN SEXUAL ELIXIR

The sexual positions, which are what comes to mind when the *Kama Sutra* is mentioned, have been selected from across all the texts and combined to provide you with variations on a pose that you can vary until you find what suits you individually. It should also be emphasized that, with sexual positions, following the spirit of the instruction is more important than getting it exactly right. Use the positions as ideas for your own sexual recipes. Think of the rooms of your home, and outdoor spaces, as your sexual playgrounds where you have complete freedom to create your own sexual elixir. It is said that the mind is where the sexual impulse originates, not in the body, which is the means of expressing your sexuality in the same way an artist uses colour. Your imagination is the most powerful instrument you can use in sexual exploration, the most basic ingredient of your sexual creativity.

Beyond the Kama Sutra is a guide to all the ingredients you need, including masturbation, oral sex, seduction, foreplay and many others, using the Eastern texts as springboards for your imagination. It simplifies what is perceived to be complicated and foreign. It is a map and a recipe book for anyone who wants to journey to the deepest levels of sexual pleasure, where you will hopefully find the most profound experience of love.

Sex and the Divine

The East, particularly India, has a long tradition of merging sexuality with the divine. Hindu deities are often paired and represent the eternal unity of male and female in sexual bliss. Hinduism teaches that self-realization, or Enlightenment, can be achieved by integrating the mind and body through many practices, including sex. The discipline of Tantra is an example of this.

Tantra as a form of sex worship goes back thousands of years and was practised by both Hindus and Buddhists, who worshipped divinities that embodied sexual energy. The acts of devotion included men performing sex with women called *vratyas*, who were considered sacred prostitutes, or transmitters of divine energy. Eventually Tantra was associated with a group of sacred writings, at the centre of which was the principle that the union of the penis (*lingam*) with the vagina (*yoni*) represented the union of cosmic powers. This meant that, through sex, the man and woman could transcend their state of separateness and become one with each other and the Divine.

WHEN EACH IS BOTH

Enlightenment, or merging into oneness to the point where 'each is both' through profound sexual experiences, may take years of practice. But, for some couples it can happen spontaneously if they are deeply in love and highly attuned to each other. In India this kind of merging would not have been expected to happen between a married couple, which is why temple prostitutes were used to perform the rite, often supervised by a guru who would ensure that it was carried out according to the scriptures.

Prostitutes served the deities at Hindu temples for centuries. Girls were given to the temple as an offering to a god, usually Krishna or Shiva, and a ritual marriage was performed that involved the loss of their virginity to a priest or a rich and powerful devotee. The girls would then be taught singing, dancing and other erotic arts that they would use during Tantric rites.

There was no equivalent male prostitute for women, as Tantrists believed that women have more spiritual energy than men, and that a man can only experience divinity through a specific type of intercourse with a woman. This involves ensuring that the woman reaches orgasm while the man does not, so that he can absorb her sexual energy. This then enables him to raise his *kundalini* energy, situated at the base of the spine, until it flows through the top of his head and connects him to the Divine. This is called *maithuna* and is similar to the Taoist practice that instructs men to refrain from ejaculating in order to conserve their life force.

Reaching orgasm is not a goal of Tantra or Taoist sexual practice. Orgasm is seen as a mere release of tension while divine ecstasy can be achieved through the pleasure of uniting your body and soul.

UNITE BODY AND SOUL THROUGH SEX

The main purpose of the *Kama Sutra*, *Ananga Ranga* and *The Perfumed Garden* is to instruct people in the ways of uniting body and soul through sex. They teach us that high-quality sex is essential to a complete experience of what it is to be human.

Wood carving of Brahma giving himself up to the cult of *lingam*.

Gods and Goddesses

Radha and Krishna languish in bed after making love.

The gods and goddesses of Hinduism offer us a variety of 'characters' that we can use to put us in touch with our own divine aspects. Each of them embodies different qualities that reflect our own personality, or traits we would like to have. Reading about them, or simply looking at pictures of them, will help us bring out those qualities in our relationships and sex lives. You will find you can go beyond the limited perceptions you have of yourself and your body.

In Tantric Hinduism, for example, Shiva was considered to be the supreme god, but his power depended on his union with Shakti, representing the female energy. It was only through his sexual

union with her that he had the power to create. Another pairing is Shiva with Kali, who is a goddess of death and destruction. However, in Hinduism this does not mean death in the literal sense, but regeneration. It is said that their love play generated such immense energy that the other gods became afraid.

KRISHNA AND RADHA

An important pair of lovers in Hinduism was Krishna and Radha. Krishna is the supreme god of the *Bhagavad Gita*, and the story tells us that Radha was the most beautiful of the *gopis*, or dairymaids, of whom Krishna was so fond that he stole their clothes when they went bathing so that he could see them naked. In descriptions of their sexual union, Radha is often portrayed as being in the woman-on-top position, and their relationship could be described as a passionate struggle. Over time Krishna devised ways to satisfy Radha and remove her jealousy while still taking care of all the other dairymaids who desired him, supposedly 900,000 of them.

BRING OUT THE GOD OR GODDESS

Using your imagination to identify with any of these lovers is fun, and can give you an idea of your own divine sexual power. Opposite is a guide to doing this for both men and women. For ease of reading, only the term 'goddess' is used. Men should substitute 'god' and think of male qualities that they admire.

Performing a Visualization

Before beginning, focus on your body. Don't look at it: close your eyes and feel it in your mind's eye. Is not the slope of your neck so graceful that it demands to be kissed and to be worshipped? And your breasts? Do they not offer visual delight? Your arms have the natural grace of a dancer and invite all into your embrace. Your thighs and legs conceal many secrets of your desires; the softness of your inner thighs longs to be kissed and to hold your lover. Experience the perfection of your body. Forget what's supposed to be beautiful and experience what is beautiful – you.

LET IT BEGIN

Now that you have experienced the beauty that is your own body, start the visualization. See yourself as you would like to. Use the images of goddesses that you find attractive and emphasize the qualities which you value and for which you would like to be known. It doesn't have to be physical beauty, it could be nurturing or fearlessness.

See all men being attracted to this aspect of you. See that they want this from you as much as they want your breasts or your sex. Feel the power that this gives you. Perhaps you have undervalued this aspect of yourself, believing it had no power of attraction.

Repeat this as often as you like, focusing on different qualities each time if you choose. Observe how people around you now respond to you as you manifest your inner goddess.

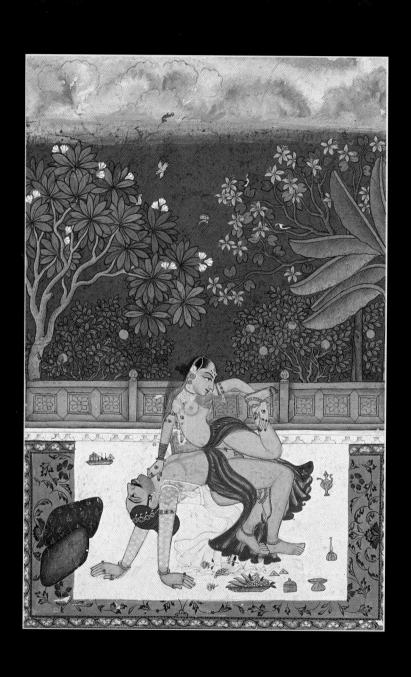

EASTERN
TRADITIONS

The 'Kama Sutra'

'Pleasures are as necessary for the well-being of the body as food'
Kama Sutra

The *Kama Sutra* is one of the oldest, and certainly the most famous, of texts devoted to the principles of sensual pleasure. It was compiled some 2,000 years ago, at the same time as the Christian gospels were being written, by Mallinaga Vatsyayana, an Indian sage who was living in the holy city of Benares.

It draws on the extensive body of Hindu erotic writings that already existed by that time. In Hinduism, sex was considered an essential part of life and therefore as worthy of study and guidance as any other aspect. Vatsyayana himself says, *'Pleasures are as necessary for the well-being of the body as food, and are consequently equally required.'*

The word 'sutra' describes spiritual teachings, often written as brief sayings. The *Kama Sutra*, as it was translated and first published in English by Sir Richard Burton's Kama Shastra Society in 1883, was composed of Vatsyayana's original sutra, plus a much later commentary on the text that gives the work substance.

In Hinduism it is considered that each person should practise *Dharma*, *Artha* and *Kama* at different times during their life to attain release from the suffering of reincarnation. Briefly, *Dharma* is following the teachings of the scriptures. *Artha* is the acquisition of knowledge, of material wealth and of a social circle. *Kama* is the enjoyment of the world using the five senses together with the mind and the soul. And this enjoyment is to be learnt from the *Kama Sutra*, or 'Science of Love'.

STUDYING THE ART OF LOVE

In its complete form, the *Kama Sutra* is a guide to mastering the senses and to healthy sexual conduct within society. The section which is drawn on here is called The Embrace. This is about sexual union itself. Here we find the types of kiss, the sex positions, and the more curious arts of scratching and biting and striking the body with passion.

Considering its antiquity and the dominance of men in most societies, it is notable that, although many men were against women studying the text, Vatsyayana encourages them and says it makes a woman more attractive if she knows the arts of love.

The *Kama Sutra* is not merely a sex manual, but also makes fascinating reading as an historical text. It is still one of the most important sources of description of physical sex, and it is as source rather than as a guide that it is best used, not least because, as some commentators point out, the instructions for sexual positions can only be followed by yoga experts with very flexible bodies. In this book, the teachings have been interpreted according to the spirit of the original rather than following it exactly. It also connects us with the lives of lovers thousands of years ago, who desired the same pleasures that we do now.

A wealthy prince pleasures the ladies of the court with this position from the *Kama Sutra*.

The 'Ananga Ranga'

This book was written by Kalyana Malla at about the same time as Columbus was discovering the Americas. It was intended not as a general guide to sexual relationships, but as a guide to sex in marriage, and was for husbands only. The *Ananga Ranga* illustrates how much society had changed since the *Kama Sutra*, with many more rigid rules in place for both sexes, but for women in particular. When Vatsyayana was writing there was no seclusion of women, and premarital and extramarital sex, while not exactly promoted, were also not prohibited.

The key purpose of the *Ananga Ranga* is to ensure that the confines of marriage do not lead to either partner becoming sexually bored by the other. At the conclusion, the author writes that: *'the chief reason for the separation between the married couple and the cause, which drives the husband to the embraces of strange women, and the wife to the arms of strange men, is the want of varied pleasures and the monotony which follows possession.'* He also says that to his knowledge nobody has written a book offering a solution to this, and so out of compassion for couples he has composed this text.

The text, the author tells us, has been written after the fashion of the Vedanta, by which he means that it can be read in two ways; as a mystical guide or as an education in the art of love. Malla, who describes himself as *'a princely sage and arch-poet'*, claims to have distilled the thoughts and writings of both holy men and poets into the work for the appreciation *'of the discerning'*.

Reflecting this combination of the mystical and the romantic, Kalyana Malla first says that the most important source of joy for mortals is knowledge of the Creator. However, the second most important source is *'the possession of a beautiful woman'*, and it is emphasized that this 'possession' takes place within marriage. The main reason he offers for the importance of marriage is the access to *'undisturbed congress'* as well as love and comfort. Although these are presented as being primarily for the benefit of men, he warns them against arrogance, because, he says, most men don't know how to make their wives sexually content, or even how to enjoy sex themselves. The reason for this is that they have not educated themselves by reading the erotic writings, and presumably here he was referring to the *Kama Sutra* amongst others.

In terms of marriage or partnership, the *Ananga Ranga* takes the view that the first, and most important step, is to find the right partner.

KEEPING LUST ALIVE

In the *Ananga Ranga*, finding a well-matched partner in terms of character, temperament, and also in terms of level of sexual appetite and preferences, is key to an enduring celebration of sexuality within a stable partnership. There is also detailed instruction in recognizing signs of indifference in a wife and what to do about it; indifference and boredom being important enemies of long-term relationships.

The author's desire is *'to prevent lives and loves being wasted'*. Through reading the book men will know *'how delicious an instrument is woman when artfully played upon ... how capable she is of producing the most exquisite harmony'* and of *'executing the most complicated variations and of giving the divinest pleasures'*. Appreciation of this and variation in the act of love is the way to keep lust alive.

A couple experimenting with erotic postures.

Tao of Loving

The great contemporary Taoist sexologist, Jolan Chang, says in *The Tao of Love and Sex* (Wildwood House, 1977) that Taoism believes, '*There can be no solution to any of the world's problems without a wholesome approach to love and sex. Nearly all destruction or self-destruction, almost all hatred and sorrow, almost all greed and possessiveness, spring from starvation of love and sex.*'

From a Taoist perspective, this is no exaggeration. Taoist physicians writing 2,000 years ago considered that sex was not just something to be enjoyed, but was also holistic and essentially life-preserving. Methods of loving were devised and written about, along with erotic pictures to aid instruction. Among these, the *Su Nu Ching* (The Classic of the Plain Girl) is considered to be one of the best. Taoism has no single text that acts as a guide. Instead, there is a set of general principles that may be applied to sex, with the three main ones being:

1. A man must find the right interval between ejaculations according to his age and his condition.
2. Ejaculation is not the pinnacle of ecstasy for a man and, that having learnt this, a man will begin to enjoy sex more wholly.
3. That female satisfaction is extremely important.

EXCHANGING YIN AND YANG

The word 'Tao' means 'the way', which is, simplistically, an awareness of the physical and non-physical world around you, and achieving a state of 'oneness' with that world. This is done by balancing the qualities of Yin and Yang. These qualities, the Taoists believed, could be observed everywhere in the natural world. Yin represents the female and Yang, the male. Yet, Yin has a little Yang, and vice versa. Humans are no different. One of the ways in which men and women can balance their own Yin and Yang energy is through sexual intercourse, when they can exchange their Yin and Yang energies. The Taoists believed that the more often people had sex, and the longer they spent engaged in it each time, the more both partners benefited in terms of health, long life and tranquility. All this in turn would contribute to a more harmonious relationship with their partner.

However, Taoists also believed that male semen was a vital essence that shouldn't be squandered if a man was to extend his life and stay healthy. It is not surprising that a culture as inventive as the Chinese found a method to deal with this that would both preserve and cultivate essential life energy. One principal solution for being able to have unlimited sex while maintaining the man's energy was to teach the ability to orgasm without ejaculation. This is also well known as a practice of Tantric sex.

UNLIMITED SEXUAL PLEASURE

The emphasis Taoists place on ejaculation control serves to enable men and women to have unlimited sexual pleasure. It also allows a man to experience several orgasms in a sex session, whereas, when ejaculation takes place, the penis has a recovery period before the man can achieve erection again. Another benefit of learning this practice is that a man can engage sexually with his partner without having to worry about whether or not he can satisfy her, as his energy levels and his capacity for maintaining an erection will be greater than those of a man who does not practise Taoist techniques.

A hidden observer is spellbound by this erotic scene from the *Tao of Love and Sex.*

The Perfumed Garden

The full title of this book is *The Perfumed Garden for the Repose of the Mind* and it was written in Tunis at the time of the Ottoman Empire by Sheikh Nefzawi. *The Perfumed Garden* uses the Arab method of story-telling to illustrate a philosophical point. Whereas the *Kama Sutra* and the *Ananga Ranga* were written from a more spiritual perspective, the writing here is erotic rather than purely instructional, and there is humour too.

The text does, of course, refer to the Islamic culture from which it originated, and Allah is praised as being the source of providing pleasure for men through the beautiful bodies of women and, for women, through men. Much of the pleasure of *The Perfumed Garden* lies in its voluptuous, poetic language which is arousing in itself and in many ways is more exciting than the actual instructions. For example, Nefzawi fulsomely describes the charms of a woman's body thus:

'He has endowed her with buttocks nobly planed, and has supported the whole on majestic thighs. Between these latter He has placed the field of strife which, when it abounds in flesh, resembles by its amplitude a lion's head. Its name among mankind is "vulva". Oh, how innumerable are the men who have died for this! How man, alas, of the bravest.'

He then describes the intoxicating powers of a woman and how men are spellbound by them. He feels it is fortunate that no man can withstand a woman's charms or free himself from the desire to possess her.

This is the most frankly sexual of all the sources, erotically written for the reader's pleasure more than for their education. The intention is to arouse through the words alone. One of the most entertaining sections of *The Perfumed Garden* is the extensive lists of names that the writer claims to have discovered for the male member and the female organs. The Shameless One and The Squeezer are but two examples:

'**The Shameless One** *It has received this name because from the minute it gets stiff and long, it cares for nobody. It unblushingly lifts its master's raiment, caring nought for the shame he feels. It acts in a shameless way with women. It will lift her clothes and expose her thighs. Its master may feel shame at its conduct but as for itself, its stiffness and ardour go on increasing.*

'**The Squeezer** *So-called because of its squeezing action on the member. Immediately after penetration it starts to squeeze the member and draws it in with such gusto that were it possible, it would absorb the testicles too.'*

Sheikh Nefzawi's view of the fun of sex is also evident in the names of the positions for coition, and reflects the overall more earthy approach of this book. Many of them are humorous, if not elegant, such as Pounding the Spot, The Stab with a Lance, and The Archimedean Screw, and sound more outrageous than they actually are.

A man and a woman engaged in erotic fulfilment.

Tantric Sex

Tantric teachings are a complete philosophy and way of life rather than being a one-off set of instructions. The word 'Tantra' is Sanskrit, meaning 'expansion', and the teachings were developed in India some time around AD 400–600. They then spread across the Indian subcontinent, travelling as far as China and Japan. There is a clear connection between Tantra and the Taoist philosophy of using sexual energy as part of spiritual development and physical health.

Tantra, in essence, is a practical way, like yoga, of developing awareness of your physical body while also teaching you how to accept your emotions, sensations and desires in a non-judgmental way. It requires patience and dedication. However, even if

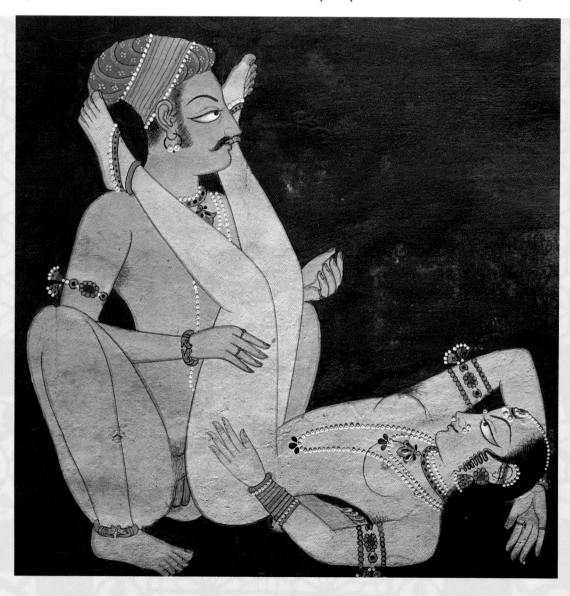

you do not want to practise Tantra with complete devotion, elements of it can still be used to enhance your sex life.

SPIRITUAL ECSTASY THROUGH SEX

Sex is one of the rituals of Tantra, and Tantrists believe that sex can awaken the *kundalini* energy stored at the base of the spine, enabling you to pull that energy up through all the chakras to the crown of the head. Once it reaches there, you experience spiritual ecstasy.

The raising of *kundalini* energy is to harmonize male and female energy. In Tantra, male energy is represented by the Hindu deity Shiva, and symbolized by the *lingam*, or penis. The essence of this male energy is the power of destruction, followed by restoration and regeneration. Destruction is not related to violent action here; it simply means to remove the old and replace it with the new, which, according the Tantra, occurs during sex. Sex removes blocks to energy and restores us to harmony and regenerates us by allowing new energy to flow through us. Sex not only gives us pleasure, it gives us healthy minds and bodies. The Shiva energy, and our conscious use of it are very important in Tantra for both enjoyment and enlightenment.

The female energy is represented by Shiva's partner, Shakti. This female energy has a range of essences and is expressed sexually in as diverse ways; nurturing, gentleness, fierceness and wildness. In Tantra, it is believed that all of us have both the Shiva and Shakti energies within us, coiled up like a serpent at the base of the spine. Sexual union is one way we can awaken these energies and express both of them, bringing them into harmony.

Through sex we are restored and regenerated while nurturing each other through loving touch and abandonment of constricting behaviour to reveal our true essence to our partner. Other ways

Amorous lovers exchange Shiva and Shakti energies during Tantric sex.

THE MELTING HUG

Include Tantra in love-making by starting with what Margot Anand, the leading writer on Tantra, calls 'The Melting Hug' (*The Art of Sexual Magic*, Piatkus, 1985). Open your arms and warmly embrace each other, without any pressure, making sure that you are touching each other at the chest, belly, pelvis and thighs. Close your eyes and breathe slowly, receiving your partner's love and feeling their warmth spread through your body. Slowly separate and make eye contact, acknowledging the love you have exchanged and which you will now create more of in the most powerful way possible: with sex.

that Tantra teaches this can be achieved is through dancing to rhythmic music, which is a wonderful prelude to sex, with the body already loosened and warmed. By contrast, another Tantric way is to use complete stillness during sex, when it is recommended you focus your awareness on your body and your partner's in order to sense the energy running between you. Repeatedly doing this will bring you more in touch with the rhythms of your sexual energy, which does not flow in a straight line to orgasm, but is like a dance.

The Japanese Art of Love

The Japanese have made some important, and visually exquisitely beautiful, contributions to erotica.

Shunga, or Images of Spring, are very highly charged and explicit erotic images, often depicting courtesans and their lovers. The courtesans were very highly prized by the Japanese men who kept them. The courtesan, like the geisha, was educated in the arts and in entertaining with music, poetry and dance. These images of courtesans and their lovers were collected together as sex manuals (*enpon*) and given to young women on their wedding night. Typically these books would depict couples engaging in a variety of sexual activities, including some 50 different positions, but would also contain information on masturbation, aphrodisiacs and sex toys. They served to both arouse and educate.

As a culture, the Japanese seem to have a much more open attitude to sex than many others. In the religious rituals of Shinto there is an emphasis on worshipping the phallus, which would explain the artists' tendency greatly to exaggerate the proportions of the male genitals in their pictures.

THE SKILL OF THE GEISHA

Geishas were not prostitutes, nor were they courtesans. Both these roles were more than adequately fulfiled by other women in certain areas of all the major cities. The areas were called the 'Floating World', and they were specifically planned into the layout of a city. There was no shame associated with visiting them. To visit a geisha, a man had to make an appointment through one of the teahouses. In the middle of the eighteenth century, Tokyo had around 3,000 women living in its Floating World.

The teahouses also offered entertainment to men who just wanted to have an afternoon or evening of relaxation. This was provided by the geishas, who were trained in the arts of singing, dancing and conversation. Although their singing and dancing could be sexually suggestive, they were not generally available for sex. If a customer wanted to have sex with a geisha he would have to negotiate with the owners of the house in which she lived. If they were agreeable he would have to take her formally as his mistress. Geishas were held in great respect and some of them became very famous, with men travelling long distances for an appointment with them.

What we can learn from them is that service is an art that, intelligently and gracefully performed, is not demeaning. The seductive techniques of the geisha are useful to us now, as they show us how to relax a man with song and dance. This need not just be the woman's role, and in a contemporary sexual relationship can be used by either partner depending on their taste and talent. Most men would enjoy watching their partners perform a dance that could then become a striptease. Others might prefer to have erotic poetry read to them, or to hear a song.

Ultimately, what Japanese erotic art and the concept of the Floating World show is that the Japanese viewed the body and sex as being part of the natural world, and that nothing in that world was sinful.

A traditional Japanese *enpon* beautifully illustrates a couple making love.

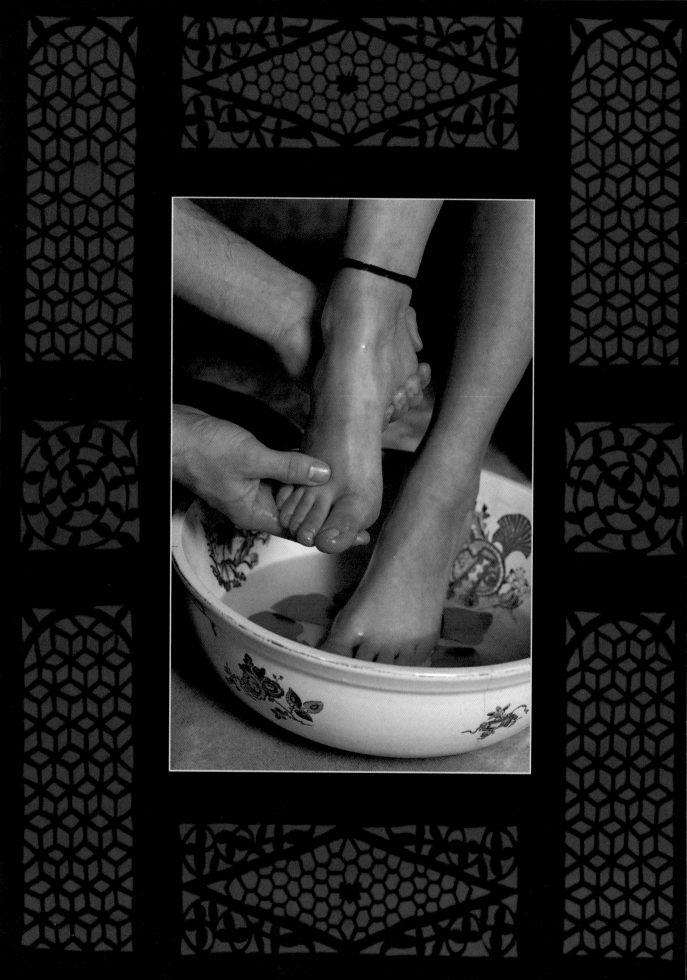

PREPARING
THE BODY

'Scents have the power of exciting sexual desires in both man and woman. When a woman inhales the scent with which a man is perfumed she loses her power of control, and it will often be found that man has here a powerful means of gaining possession of a woman.'
The Perfumed Garden

Our natural body scent is one of the most intoxicating, and contains pheromones that are an integral part of sexual attraction. While other scents can play a part in our love making, it is the clean, natural body that is the most arousing.

Bathing

'Now the man should wash his teeth, apply a limited quantity of ointments and perfumes to his body, put some ornaments on his person and collyrium on his eyelids and below his eyes, colour his lips and look at himself in the glass. They should bathe amidst the sounds of auspicious musical instruments, they should decorate themselves and dine together.' Kama Sutra

Across all cultures, the public bath house has had, and in some continues to have, an important place in society, associated with all kinds of rituals. The Japanese have perhaps the most beautiful public bathing places that incorporate hot springs as well as their traditional deep tubs. Geishas, and wives, would ladle warm water over the men, in an act that symbolizes devotion. Bathing together, or bathing your partner, is an intimate way to commence love making, as you will both feel fresh and your bodies will be more relaxed.

SANCTUARY AND RENEWAL

In many homes the bathroom has become a place of sanctuary. What better place to commence an evening of love by washing the day off yourself and your partner? There are several ways to go about this, and the one you choose should fit the mood of both of you.

Sometimes all that is wanted is the speed and simplicity of sharing a warm shower or bath. At other times you will feel like creating an erotic atmosphere in your bathroom with candles and scents, maybe taking a bottle of wine or champagne in with you and lingering together in the bath, talking.

Providing pampering, as the geisha does, without seeking it for yourself, is an essential part of a sexual relationship. It is expressed in sex when one partner pleasures the other without asking for any pleasure in return – the giving is sufficient in itself. Imagine yourself coming home stressed after a difficult day and finding that you had nothing to do except let the bad feelings go. Your partner is there to help you. The bathroom is candlelit, the water is scented, the room is warm, you slip into the water and they hand you a drink. You can talk, and they listen as they ladle the water over your body. Let your partner massage your head while they shampoo your hair, moving the scalp with their fingers in a circular motion over the head. There is the possibility of

massage and of sex. Allow your partner to dry you, and indulge yourself in childhood memories of someone taking care of you.

SENSUAL WARM WATER

If you choose to bathe together, sink into the sensual experience of your bodies in warm water. Wash each other slowly and carefully with soap, leaving the genital areas until last. Allow the sexual tension to build up in this way. This is another way of mutually masturbating each other, as the water and soap provides a pleasing lubricant for both of you, and reaching a climax in water is another experience to add to your repertoire. You can also play in the water, splash each other and have a laugh: one of the great tension-reducers.

The occasion can be as simple or as stylish as you wish. It can be a prelude to an evening of sex or an intimate moment to be relished and enjoyed for its own sake.

Perfumes and Oils

'Fill the tent with delicious perfumes of various kinds, amber, musk, and scented flowers such as the rose, orange blossom, jonquil, jasmine, hyacinth and others similar.' The Perfumed Garden

Eastern cultures, particularly those of Arabia, have a long tradition of associating scent with sensuality.

The *Ananga Ranga* suggests sprinkling the bed with rose water and flower petals, and burning woody incense, while the *Kama Sutra* says the room should be balmy with rich perfumes. Fresh flowers may not always be an option, but you can achieve similar sensual effects with essential oils.

CHOOSING THE RIGHT OIL

To create the right ambience, choose oils that are relaxing, warming and aphrodisiac.

ROSE OIL immediately connects us to images of love and sensuousness, and it is known to be an aphrodisiac with an added tonic effect.

YLANG YLANG is an exotic Far Eastern scent that calms the nerves and lifts bad moods. It has quite a heavy, sweet scent, so use it sparingly.

FRANKINCENSE is at the other end of the scent spectrum, with a spicy, woody aroma that may be more appealing to a man.

Other oils for sensual use are:

GERANIUM (floral) – a tonic with sedative qualities that reduces anxiety.

JASMINE (floral) – a mood lifter with strong aphrodisiac effects.

JUNIPER (woody) – stimulating and relaxing. Good for lack of energy.

LAVENDER (floral) – stimulating and relaxing.

PATCHOULI (woody) – an earthy aromatic that can either stimulate or act as a sedative depending on how much is used.

SANDALWOOD (woody) – enhances sexual awareness.

How you and your partner use these will depend on your scent preferences. They are simple to use and will benefit your mood and your libido.

CREATING THE PERFECT ATMOSPHERE

Burn essential oils to scent a room or add them to a carrier oil for application to the body. One or two drops of each essential oil is usually sufficient to achieve the scent and effects you want. Essential oils have the potential to be powerful mood changers and some people are more sensitive to them than others. Always use them in a carrier oil, such as almond, avocado or wheatgerm, in the proportion of 1:50, never directly on the skin. Scent a room with oils using an oil burner (never let it burn dry), a plastic plant spray (add 5 drops of oil to 600ml of warm water), or a few drops in a bowl of water near a radiator; or place drops of your favourite oil on a ceramic ring that fits around a light bulb.

Hair

One of the reasons some religions demand that women cover their hair, revealing it only to their husband, is that it is believed to be the centrepiece of their beauty, or *'crowning glory'*. Also, because the hair grows from the head, which is the part of the body closest to heaven, it is thought to be the dwelling place of the soul.

The ancient Hindus believed that the forces of creation could be unleashed through a woman's hair. They also believed that the fearsome goddess Kali could create thunderstorms by unbinding her hair; these storms only calmed when she combed her hair and bound it up again. Shiva is always depicted with wild, long hair said to represent the creative and sexual energy of the universe.

Don't underestimate the eroticism of the smell and feel of just-washed hair, especially if you have long hair that you can trail over your partner's face or body. It is deeply intimate to let your partner wash your hair for you and can be seen as a powerful element of foreplay. Combing each other's hair and massaging the head and neck are simple but exquisite ways of combining tenderness with sexuality, and can be an intimate and erotic experience for both lovers.

HAIR AND SEX PLAY

The *Ananga Ranga* deals extensively with using hair as part of sexual activity. At the time the text was written, all women had long hair. The text itself says that: *'Ideally, the woman's hair should be soft, close, thick, black and wavy.'*

The *Ananga Ranga* suggests:
'Softly hold and handle the hair when the woman wakes. This is said to kindle hot desire.

The man holds the woman's hair between his two palms at the back of her head, at the same time kissing her lower lip.

The man holds the woman's hair and uses it to gently pull her towards him for a kiss.

The last is when during coition the man holds the woman's hair on both sides of her head, just above the ears, and she does the same to him, while they both exchange many kisses.'

INDIAN HEAD MASSAGE

Another way of including hair in your sex play is to massage the hair. Indian head massage is an art that relieves stress and helps relaxation. Follow the hairline round and pay attention to where the skull meets the neck. Use circular movements all over, followed by tapping all over gently with the tips of your fingers as this helps to stimulate the blood circulation. Alternate the circular massage movements with the tapping ones. You could use oils in your partner's hair while you are massaging and then shampoo them out afterwards, making it an even more sensual experience.

Hands and Feet

'The man should place his hands between her thighs, upon her breasts, which she would probably cover with her own hands.' Kama Sutra

'A praiseworthy woman will have hands and feet that are noticeable for their elegance.' The Perfumed Garden

THE POWER OF HANDS

Our hands are the means by which we make physical contact and thus are the most important tools in our relationships. Lovers build up a complete private vocabulary of touch over time, and the most simple of them, such as a hand on the back, can convey emotions more effectively than a few words.

Hands are also healing, and even if you are not a trained healer your touch can be powerful: stroking the forehead can alleviate a headache; a hand placed on the stomach can take away pain. Giving your lover a massage is a powerful way of communicating, especially when you allow your emotions to flow through your hands.

Gestures with your hands are also powerful forms of non-verbal communication. In Indian and Arabic dancing, the movement of the hands is used to express emotional and sexual messages to the audience.

Keep your hands clean and well tended, just as you would other parts of your body. Make them look as attractive and soft as possible. Try to be more conscious of the gestures you make with your hands, and of the intent with which you touch.

EROTIC FEET

Feet have also been fetish objects in many cultures. The sight of a woman's foot in a high heel is a sexual turn-on for a considerable number of men, not least because it suggests vulnerability.

The foot can be used erotically. Decorating them, as Indian women do with henna, toe rings

and ankle bracelets, as well as the more conventional pedicure, both draw attention to the sexuality of the feet. A man can use his big toe to stimulate the clitoris, but this will only be a pleasure if his feet are cared for. One way to ensure this is to pamper his feet yourself. Washing the feet is a very powerful act of devotion in both the East and West. Massage them with scented oils. Doing this for each other is a powerful way of showing acceptance and love. It is also extremely relaxing and sensuous for most people, but be aware that not all people like it. Taking care of your partner's feet is a way of symbolizing that you care about how they move through the world, which is what partnership is essentially about.

IN TOUCH WITH TOUCH

Try this playful exercise as a way of becoming more conscious of your touch. Don't take it too seriously. Have fun with it and hopefully you will learn at the same time. Take turns and let your partner touch you too.

Ask your partner to undress, keeping warm and comfortable. Now pick a part of their body, and with a specific emotional intention, touch them in a way you think conveys this. Repeat it a few times, and then ask your partner what they feel when you do it. Are they getting your message, or are you getting your wires crossed? Vary the types of touch you use, and include tickling.

SEDUCTION

*'Women being of a tender nature want tender beginnings, and when
they are forcibly approached by men with whom they are but slightly
acquainted they sometimes become haters of sexual connection, and
sometimes even haters of the male sex. The man should therefore
approach the girl according to her liking, and should make use of
those devices by which he may be able to establish
himself more and more into her confidence.'*

Kama Sutra

Preparing the Place and Setting the Mood

'Choose the largest, finest and most airy room in the house, purify it thoroughly with whitewash and decorate its spacious and beautiful walls with pictures and other objects upon which the eye may dwell with delight. Wall lights should gleam around the hall reflected by a hundred mirrors whilst both the man and woman should contend against any reserve or false shame, giving themselves up to unrestrained voluptuousness.' Ananga Ranga

INSPIRATION FOR SEDUCTION

Seduction is whatever inspires us to lust, and while some accuse it of causing the downfall of strong men and vulnerable women, it is praised as the secret weapon of legendary lovers by others. There is a sense of intentionally drawing your lover away from the everyday world and into a state of arousal through pleasuring all the senses.

Seduction is an art form, a performance from the heart that encompasses everything from the most elaborate scene-setting to a quickie in the kitchen. It is love play that indulges and stretches your imagination and perhaps most importantly, it is a gift of desire and pleasure to your lover. When that is your intention it isn't difficult to become an accomplished seducer or seductress.

When it comes to seduction, it is easy to opt for a few tried and tested routines. The candlelit dinner is a favourite one; the bottle of wine in front of a roaring fire is another. Certainly you may want to eat, but neither the dinner nor the candles are the keys to seduction. They are just theatrical props. For a heightened experience of pleasure, take these props and weave them into a more personal story of which you are the author. Your aim is to seduce your lover into the role you have imagined for them, and to ensure they enjoy it as much as you do.

THE PROMISE OF PLEASURE TO COME

Remember that seduction doesn't have to be a big gesture; it can start with a small one such as a foot massage at the end of a hard day. It can be exchanged glances, subtle comments, or the briefest touch that promises pleasure later, enforced delay being a delightful ingredient of seduction. Whatever seduction technique you use, and variety is vital, it will be successful if you enter into it with love and lust.

Food for Love

'Provide refreshments such as cocoa-nut, betel leaf and milk which is so useful for retaining and restoring vigour.'

'When the girl accepts the embrace, the man should put a tambula, or screw of betel nut and betel leaves in her mouth.'

'They should bathe amidst the sounds of auspicious musical instruments, should decorate themselves and dine together.' Kama Sutra

EAT FOR AROUSAL

Some foods are associated with love and sex, particularly fruits – with their colours and fleshy textures which symbolize the body and the genitals. The fig, for example, when cut open is like the vulva, while the banana has obvious connotations.

Eating fruits or vegetables like asparagus or artichokes also mimics sexual acts. They require you to suck and the juice runs down your face. It can be very erotic to watch your partner eat like this as it suggests that this is how they will enjoy your body. The Chinese valued pomegranates for being symbolic of fertility, while the Arabs thought that the aroma of almonds induced passion.

Sexual stamina, too, has long been associated with eating certain foods. To *'keep the penis so hard you might think it will never return to a flaccid state'*, cook eggs with myrhh, cinnamon and pepper. To *'keep a penis erect day and night'*, simply enjoy a regular drink of camel's milk mixed with honey. So advises *The Perfumed Garden*.

FOOD FOR LOVE

When planning a sensual meal together, choose foods that look enticing and can be lingered over. Greece and the Middle East have many dishes that lend themselves to this sort of languorous consumption: dips like hummus and tzatziki, salads like tabbouleh, and falafel, prawns or grilled chicken. Dip bread into olive oil and have a selection of cheeses surrounded by seductive fruits like strawberries, dates, grapes, mangos and figs. Vanilla deserves a special mention as its scent and

flavour is thought to increase lust. Try adding part of a vanilla pod to a glass of champagne.

Eat with your fingers. This enhances your sensual contact with the food. It is also infinitely pleasing to eat something off your partner's fingers, and you can suggestively suck and lick their fingers clean afterwards. If you eat naked, food can be eaten off your partner's body. Make your partner lie still while you decorate their body with a selection of morsels. Then eat them very slowly, finishing off with plenty of sucking, kissing and licking.

Lastly, prepare food together whenever you can. This doesn't have to be part of the prelude to sex, just part of your togetherness. But do it mindfully. Touch each other as you pass, exchange a kiss and above all be playful and you will nourish each other emotionally as well as nutritionally.

Music, Dance and Poetry

'Scattered about this room place musical instruments, especially the pipe and lute, also books containing amorous songs with illustrations of love postures.'

'She is fond of pleasure and variety: she delights in singing and in every kind of accomplishment, especially the manual arts.' Ananga Ranga

TITILLATE WITH VERSE

One of the easiest ways of adding art to your seduction scene is to read poetry to your lover. Chinese and Japanese erotic poetry collections are widely available and are highly suggestive. This fourth-century poem by Tzu Yuh, for example, could start the mind racing:

In this house on a hill without walls,
The four winds touch our faces.
If they blow open your robe of gauze,
I'll try to hide my smile.

The idea is to use the poetry to stimulate your lover's imagination, so if possible choose poems with images that reflect your own desires. Add some erotic and spiritual love poems by the Persian poets Rumi and Kabir, and those by ancient Indian poets such as Bihari and Mirabai. Finally, one lasting seductive gift to your lover would be a poem written by you.

TANTALIZE WITH SONG

Music stirs our emotions and heightens them at amazing speed. We often associate a specific song with a significant life event, and many couples have what they refer to as 'their song'.

Most of us can sing. You might not have perfect pitch, but that isn't necessary for singing a simple song to your lover. It is the creative expression of you that your partner will find enchanting and sensuous. The types of music that excite us sexually are very individual, and only you will know what works for you and your partner. What better excuse for trying out all kinds of music than finding the sound that turns you both on?

SEDUCE WITH DANCE

Music is also about dance. This is perhaps an easier way to seduce your lover, because you can dance *with* them if you don't feel daring enough to dance *for* them.

Most men are excited by the prospect of a woman performing some kind of erotic dance for them, so if you find it too difficult to do it in your own persona, dress up a little and imagine you are an exotic Eastern belly dancer. Dance rhythmically in front of him, moving up close and, as he is about to touch you, pull away. Let him admire your body in graceful movement. Lose yourself in the dance and abandon your inhibitions. If you remove them here there will be fewer of them in bed. Get lost in the music and let him savour your body as it moves just for him. Allow your hips and breasts to move. Go right up to him and let him admire you all round. Get close to him, then pull away. Maybe you have a scarf you could throw to him. At the end invite him to dance with you. Pull him close so your hips fit close together. Hold your lips up to be kissed, and take it from there.

Signs of Arousal

'As soon as she commences to enjoy pleasure the eyes are half closed and watery; the body waxes cold; the breath after being hard and jerky is expired in sobs or sighs, the lower limbs are limply stretched out after a period of rigidity... then the wise know, that the paroxysm having taken place, the woman has enjoyed plenary satisfaction.' Ananga Ranga

Lovers need to be aware of the signs, especially the subtle ones, that communicate the desire for sex. The Eastern texts all explore learning the signs of arousal and orgasm, mainly those shown by women (they were mostly written for male readers). Arousal is harder to detect in a woman than in a man, and the sources all agree that women are generally slower to become aroused.

READ THE SIGNS

It is true that women usually, but not always, need more preparation for sex than men do. The only truly reliable guide to the level of arousal is the woman herself. However, observing the woman's unconscious body movements will help her partner to be more sensitive to her arousal. The *Kama Sutra* keeps it simple:

'Her body relaxes, she closes her eyes, she puts aside all bashfulness, and shows increased willingness to unite the two organs as closely as possible.'

Somewhat more specific is the *Ananga Ranga*, which describes arousal to orgasm like this:

'She rubs and repeatedly smoothes her hair. She strokes her own cheeks. She draws her dress over her bosom, apparently to readjust it, but leaves her breasts partly exposed. She bites her lower lip. She stammers, and does not speak clearly and distinctly.

She sighs and sobs without reason. She even throws herself in her husband's way and will not readily get out of his path.'

The *Tao* gives the most explicit account of the different stages of arousal in a woman and how they progress to orgasm:

'The 10 Stages of Loving
1. *She holds her man tight with both hands, indicating that she wants closer body contact.*
2. *She raises her legs, showing that she wants clitoral stimulation.*
3. *She extends her abdomen, which shows that she wants shallower thrusts.*
4. *She moves her thighs, showing that she is greatly pleased.*
5. *She pulls the man closer with her feet, to show she wants deeper thrusts.*
6. *She crosses her legs over his back, indicating that she wants more.*
7. *She shakes from side to side, showing that she wants her man to make deep thrusts on each side.*
8. *She lifts her body, showing that she is enjoying it extremely.*
9. *She relaxes her body, indicating that her body and limbs are pacified.*
10. *Her vulva floods, her Yin has come. She is happy.'*

FOREPLAY

*'Know, oh Vizier that if you wish to experience an agreeable
copulation, one that gives equal satisfaction and pleasure to both
parties, it is necessary to frolic with the woman and excite her with
nibbling, kissing and caressing until you see by her eyes that
the moment of pleasure has arrived...then is the time to
get between her thighs and penetrate her...'*
The Perfumed Garden

*'The vulva is the swing in which the Love God rides. Opened with two
fingers, it causes the love juice to flow. The Sunshade of the Love God
is placed just above the entrance of the God's dwelling. Not far from it
is the Full Moon duct, and when these three zones are rubbed with the
finger, the woman is brought into condition.'*
Kama Sutra

Kissing

'When a kiss is given by husband to wife, or wife to husband if he be cleanshaven, both lips of one are taken and pressed between the lips of the other, it is the closed kiss (sampata). This becomes tongue wrestling when their two tongues meet and struggle with each other.' Ananga Ranga

In the build up to the first sexual contact with a lover, it is the anticipation of the opening kiss that draws us in. Our eyes are drawn to the other's lips again and again, sending signals that we are ready and willing to give and receive a kiss. It is that first kiss that tells us if we want another. In a matter of seconds all our senses have taken in and digested an enormous amount of information about the other person. This will be reduced to a simple message: if the kiss is pleasing we will want more.

KISSING IS THE KEY TO AROUSAL

An essential element of foreplay, kissing should be continued throughout love making. As *The Perfumed Garden* says, '*Any posture is unsatisfactory if kissing is impossible.*' In the *Tao of Loving*, the importance of kissing is placed second only to the act of coition, as it was believed that the man and woman could receive each other's Yin and Yang essences through the kiss, while the *Kama Sutra* and *Ananga Ranga* describe the different types of kiss in detail, showing that kissing was recognized as key to intimate arousal.

The *Kama Sutra* describes the different types of kissing at length and says: '*The following are the places for kissing: the forehead, the eyes, the cheeks, the throat, the bosom, the breasts, the lips and the interior of the mouth.*' It then goes on to describe the four styles of kissing – moderate, contracted, pressed and soft which should be used according to the body part that is being kissed.

According to the *Kama Sutra*, the four main types of kisses are:
'THE STRAIGHT KISS – *when the lips of two lovers are brought into direct contact.*
'THE BENT KISS – *when the heads of two lovers are bent towards each other, and when so bent, kissing takes place.*
'THE TURNED KISS – *when one of them turns up the face of the other by holding the head and chin and then kisses them.*
'THE PRESSED KISS – *when the lower lip is pressed with much force.*'

The Taoists believed that the saliva of a sexually aroused woman could strengthen a man's life force and blood if he swallowed it, which is one of the reasons why they held kissing to be such an important element of love making. Called Jade Spring, it was considered to be one of the three important female secretions, the others being White Snow (from the breasts) and Moon Flower Water (from the womb). There is a Tantric technique for collecting this saliva, which is produced under the tongue at the point of orgasm. As orgasm approaches, the woman places her tongue on the roof of her mouth, then as she climaxes she offers her partner her tongue to suck on.

Varying the pressure of your kisses, spending more time kissing, and perhaps trying different types of kisses, such as erotic kissing (see page 50), will harmonize your levels of arousal, and can be enjoyed for themselves.

Erotic Kissing

'This is done by the wife, who, excited with passion, covers her husband's eyes with her hands, and closing her husband's eyes with her hands, and closing her own eyes, thrusts her tongue into his mouth, moving it to and fro with a motion so pleasant and slow that it at once suggests another and higher form of enjoyment.' Ananga Ranga

Our lips and tongues are erotic organs resembling the vaginal orifice and the phallus. Unlike the genitals, our lips, mouths and tongues do not tire so easily. This means that kissing can continue long after the genitals have grown tired. Also, while resting after sex, continuing with kissing can arouse your partner to desire again. Particularly good for this is a form of kiss taught by the Tantric tradition, which says that a woman's upper lip is

connected to her palate and her clitoris. So, sucking or nibbling the woman's upper lip subtly arouses her by stimulating the clitoris. This is echoed in the *Kama Sutra* in The Kiss of the Upper Lip, when the man kisses the woman's upper lip while she kisses his lower lip. There is also The Greatly Pressed Kiss, when the lower lip is pressed with some force and then touched with the tongue.

SOFTLY, SOFTLY

The tongue should always be tentatively introduced into kissing until you know how it is being received. If you are mindful of the fact that the tongue is like a penis, then you will understand the need for patience when using it in kissing. The tongue can be used to explore male and female roles, the active and passive, if you are both aware that you are using your lips and tongues to symbolize the genitals. Taking it in turns to use your tongues, and to bite and suck on each other's lips, is a very sensual and erotic form of mutual exploration.

Ultimately, the secret of good kissing is to enjoy it and to keep the mouth, the tongue and the facial muscles relaxed. This will increase your receptivity to your lover's lips. A tight-lipped kiss is a turn-off, and as the Taoists believed, speaks volumes about a person's personality and sexual characteristics. All the sources agree, though, that the arousal of being well kissed is essential to full enjoyment of coition.

Sensual Touch and Massage

'The room, balmy with rich perfumes, should contain a bed covered with a clean white cloth, flowers upon it and a canopy above it, and two pillows, one at the top, another at the bottom. There should be a couch besides and a stool on which should be placed the fragrant ointments for the night.' Kama Sutra

'Prepare a mixture of honey and ginger, rubbing it in sedulously. Then let him join the woman and he will procure for her such pleasure that she objects to him getting off her.' The Perfumed Garden

The importance of kissing and caressing your lover's body is emphasized in all the Eastern texts, and the art of massage was undoubtedly practised by the people of those cultures. Massaging your lover on a regular basis is a loving way to show devotion and service to them.

PREPARING FOR A MASSAGE

Where you choose to give a massage is up to you. Your bedroom is probably the most intimate: put a quilt on the floor and cover it with a towel. Make sure the room is warm and have extra towels to cover the parts of the body on which you are not working. The body loses heat quickly when it is lying still and relaxed. Create an erotic mood with soft lighting or candles, scented oils and some relaxing music.

It is most pleasant if the massage oil is slightly warmed before use. You can do this in an oil burner, but make sure it doesn't get too hot. Even if it is warm, do not pour the oil directly onto your partner's body. Instead, pour it into your hands and stroke your palms together so that they are covered. Then apply the oil to the body. You should be able to glide your hands over your partner's body without any friction.

MASSAGING THE BACK

This is where most massage begins. You may prefer to kneel at the side, or to straddle your partner's buttocks. Remember always to massage upwards and out, moving your hands in the direction of the heart at all times.

Applying the oil, place your hands on either side of the spine, below the waist, and massage upwards and out towards the sides. Keep the strokes firm and sweeping without jerky movements. Work your way up to the shoulders, the strokes becoming longer as you sweep your hands up from the lower back to the base of the neck.

Move your hands out along both shoulders and then lightly glide your hands down your partner's side until they are in the starting position. Repeat

this several times. If there are points on the back that feel knotted, rub them with your thumb pad or middle finger in a circular motion until they soften and disappear.

SHIATSU FOR SEXUAL ENERGY

The kidney region is our source of sexual energy. Working here with finger pressure will improve the libido. Once you have finished massaging the back, place your hands on either side of the spine over both kidneys. Make small circling or pumping motions with your thumbs over the area. Alternatively, press on a single spot and then release the pressure, working your way around the kidneys.

MASSAGING THE BUTTOCKS

The buttocks are full of nerve endings, so having them massaged is especially pleasurable.

Place your fingertips at the top of the buttocks and work downwards, kneading with your palms. Work the outsides of the buttocks in a downwards motion, ending with your wrists meeting at the base of the cheeks. Hold the cheeks together.

Now work upwards, using the same movements and firm pressure, finishing with your fingertips in the starting position.

MASSAGING ARMS AND HANDS

Applying more oil, start with long sweeping strokes from the shoulder to the hand. Hold your partner's hand in yours and gently tug each of the fingers and the thumb, one by one. Turn the hand palm upwards and massage the palm in a circular motion using your thumb pad.

Now circle the arm with your hand and use a 'squeeze and move up' technique until you reach the top of the arm. Then use the flat of your hand to stroke downwards. Repeat this several times before moving to the other arm and hand. Finish off both arms with feathery downward strokes as far as the fingertips.

SHIATSU FOR FERTILITY AND SEXUAL ENERGY

Use thumb pressure or small circling motions of the thumb on the area called the 'greater stream', which is a point between the ankle bone and the Achilles tendon. This will improve sexual energy in men and aid fertility in women. Another point that can be pressed with the tips of the fingers to help fertility is the meeting point of the 'Yin leg meridians' which is about four finger-widths above the ankle bone on the outer leg.

MASSAGING LEGS AND FEET

Use the heel of your hand to stroke down firmly the instep from toes to heel. Return your hand to the ball of the foot in a single stroke and repeat several times. Work from the heel to the toes using circular movements of your thumb. Rotate the ankle gently in both directions. Flex the toes back and forth gently, then gently tug each toe, as you did with the fingers, slightly rotating them as you do this.

Work your way up the inner legs to the groin, using the same type of stroke as you used on the back. Now repeat this on the outside of the legs. You can repeat both of these movements several times. Now work on the upper thighs using the kneading movement you used on the buttocks. Finish with feathery strokes down the legs from hip to toe.

MASSAGING THE CHEST

Working from behind your partner's head, use sweeping, circular strokes across the whole chest, starting from the centre. Using the heels of your hand, make smaller circular movements across the upper chest, especially around the collar bone. Repeat the strokes across the whole chest, now sweeping up to the shoulders.

Place your hands on the shoulders, with your thumbs underneath, and draw the thumbs up towards you, lifting and squeezing the muscles gently. Finish with light, feathery strokes across the chest and shoulders. Complete the massage with a little attention to the head and forehead. Circular motions, like those used in shampooing, will leave your partner feeling relaxed from top to toe.

SHIATSU TO RELEASE ENERGY

Tiredness can depress sexual energy. About four finger-widths beneath the navel sits the 'gate to the original chi'. Light pressure on this point will help to release any stuck energy. Likewise, there is a point about two thumb-widths on either side of the navel that will help to relieve menstrual problems.

Tao of Masturbation

'The women of the royal harem, having dressed the daughters of their nurses, or their female friends, or their female attendants like men, they accomplish their object by means of bulbs, roots and fruits having the form of the lingam, or they lie down upon the statue of a male figure on which the lingam is visible and erect.' Kama Sutra

In ancient cultures, particularly in Egypt, India and China, women were taught techniques for circulating sexual energy around their bodies. Using these techniques encouraged women to make use of their sexual energy first for themselves and second in relationships. The oriental philosophies, such as Taoism, didn't see sexual energy as being related just to sex; they believed that it was an important element of our physical and mental health.

Below is a simple exercise, based on Taoist principles, that will help you to experience your sexual energy as an energy that pervades your entire body and increases your mental creativity and your sexual desire.

BREATHING IN PLEASURE

Use the breathing technique described here during masturbation to increase your feelings of pleasure and to learn what gives you pleasure. Remember that, every time you breathe out, you are breathing out fear. When you breathe in, focus on the pleasurable sensations in your body. As you feel yourself approach orgasm, use your breath to take you into it, breathing past any emotional blocks that are holding you back. In this way you move out of your head and into your body.

Make sure you have a quiet place to practise where you will not be disturbed. You can do the exercise sitting or lying down.

Begin by exhaling through your nose. At the end of the out breath, tighten your stomach muscles and flatten your abdomen slightly. You will feel your diaphragm muscle push up as you do this, squeezing the air up and out of you. Push as much air out as you can, without unnaturally forcing it, until your lungs are empty. By relaxing the stomach muscles, you will breathe in naturally and bring the air down into the abdomen so that it swells up. Again, don't force this or you will create tension, which will destroy the effect.

Once your abdomen feels full of air, exhale again. Repeat three times at first. When you are comfortable with the technique, you can increase the repetitions.

When you feel confident with this technique you might like to try it with your partner. Ask them to stimulate you while you focus on your breathing and your body sensations. This is a lovely way of sharing and creating intimacy.

Fantasy and Role Play

'Variety is necessary in love, so love is to be produced by means of variety. It is on this account that courtesans who are well acquainted with the various ways and means become so desirable, for if variety is sought in all the arts and amusements, how much more should it be sought after in love.' Kama Sutra

Fantasies of any kind are an expression of our creativity. They are a healthy part of our sexuality, and when two people feel safe in sharing their fantasies, they reinforce their bonds and add an important stimulus to their relationship.

Playing out your fantasy life with a partner is sexually intoxicating. It is also personally powerful in that, through it, you can present parts of your persona that may normally be hidden. For you and your partner this is a real opportunity for revelation as well as pleasure. There are many ways to enjoy fantasy and role play.

ROLE-PLAY GAMES

The forbidden lure of the harem and the seduction from it of one of the ruler's women is an enduring fantasy. Another is the geisha who is serving a client and who is then seduced by him into having sex, just as he is seduced by her demure demeanour and her artistic talents.

Harem Seclude yourself in the bathroom and fill a bath with jasmine and ylang ylang oils. Turn off the lights and burn candles. You are alone and naked. Outside the door is a guard who will prevent you from being disturbed, and who is also preventing you from escaping. You are relaxed, stroking your own body, perhaps masturbating because you have not been sexually satisfied for some time. Suddenly, a man enters the bathroom. You cannot cover yourself, and indeed have no wish to. He holds your hands away from your body, substituting one of his, with which he

caresses your breasts at the same time as sucking them. He tells you that he has come to take you away and pulls you, willingly, out of the bath. He dries you, picks you up and takes you to the bedroom (which is his palace) where your passion builds together until you joyfully surrender to him sexually.

Geisha Prepare some foods and drink that can be served by hand to the man's mouth. Play some soft music and bring out a bowl of scented water in which to wash his feet and a warm, soft towel to dry them, as well as some lotion to rub into them afterwards. Wear light, soft clothing that can be easily removed. Tend to him and from time to time let him catch a glimpse of your breasts, shoulder or thighs. Look at him from under your eyelashes.

The man might then try to touch you, and at first you pull away. He might ask you to remove his shirt so you can massage his neck and back, which you do. He will now find a reason to remove his trousers. He will have an erection that he needs you to massage. What he asks you to do next is up to him, but as geisha you must respond to his requests, although you may demand something in return for your service. That is up to your imagination...

ROLE-PLAY RULES

Sex is a natural ending to role play – after that you can drop your 'identities'. Don't discuss what you have done afterwards. The magic was in the moment, so don't shatter it with doubts or fear. Use the emotional and physical memory of it for future sexual arousal.

ORAL SEX

Oral sex requires us to get up close and personal. It is one of the
most sexually gratifying acts for men and women of any age and
physical ability, and many people create a satisfying sex life
with oral sex at its centre.

*'The acts that are done on the jaghana or middle parts of women, are done
in the mouths of these eunuchs, and this is called Auparishtaka.'*
Kama Sutra

The Kama Sutra of Mouth Congress

The Taoists believed that the man could direct energy into his partner's body through the tongue, and in turn could receive her Moon Flower Water as she climaxed. This was one way to exchange their Yin/Yang essence.

Oral sex is prominently absent from all the ancient texts with the exception of the *Kama Sutra*. Indeed, Vatsyayana is not exactly in favour of it and only writes primarily about fellatio, which was an aspect of the art of massage and usually performed between men.

There is no mention of men performing oral sex on their wives, although it is clear that men practised it on women of the harem and that, within the harem, women performed cunnilingus on each other.

However, oral sex is a key part of contemporary sex. There are just two basic rules that need to be observed to obtain the most pleasure: cleanliness and respecting boundaries.

While natural odour is exciting, cleanliness is a courtesy to your partner. Bathing together beforehand can be titillating and ensures you both feel comfortable. That said, the salty, musky tastes and smells of sexual secretions are biochemically designed to arouse us, so get used to the scent of your own arousal, and it will help you to take pleasure in and have confidence during any sex, but particularly oral. Men find the scent of a woman's sexual secretions extremely arousing, and love to smell and taste it. When he offers you a kiss on the lips after oral sex, relish it and enjoy sharing your smell and taste with him.

COMMUNICATION IS VITAL

Oral sex requires you to be more vulnerable. For some this adds to the excitement, while for others it makes it very frightening. Communicating your likes and dislikes is very important. It is clearly wrong to assume that what sent a previous partner to the heights of ecstasy will work for your present one. At the beginning of a new relationship you may be nervous about telling your lover that their technique is not arousing you but, if you don't, frustration will build up, followed possibly by resentment that could cause the end of the relationship. The saying 'different strokes for different folks' is particularly applicable to oral sex.

If oral sex just doesn't appeal to you at all, don't feel that you have to include it. You can still have a rich and satisfying sex life without it.

Cunnilingus

'Now spread, indeed cleave asunder, that archway with your nose and let your tongue gently probe her yoni *(vagina), with your nose, lips and chin slowly circling: it becomes* Jihva-bhramanaka *(The Circling Tongue).'* Kama Sutra

In ancient Eastern traditions the vulva was considered a sacred part of the body. A woman who opens herself up to her partner by allowing him to perform cunnilingus is offering him a most intimate part of herself.

PERFECTING THE TECHNIQUE

Kissing the mouth is a good way to practise for oral sex, running your tongue around the outer lips and then between them. This will give you an idea of the amount of pressure your partner likes. Being prepared to take time over this is another prerequisite, especially if you want to bring your partner to orgasm. The best lovers make it clear that time is immaterial and that their partner may take as long as they wish to climax. The man should also communicate the fact that he is enjoying giving pleasure.

Begin by working your way down the woman's body. Make her feel safe by starting at her mouth, then move to her breasts. Spend time on sucking and licking the breasts as that will excite the genitals. Kiss the belly, and then the pubic mound, gently parting her legs and kissing the outer lips of the vulva.

'LAP HER LOVER-WATER'

Part the outer lips and look at the entrance to the vagina and clitoris. Begin with some light strokes with your tongue over the clitoris to see how your partner reacts. The clitoris is extremely sensitive and some women cannot stand direct stimulation of it. Use your tongue on the underside of the clitoris and around the side of it. Use a flicking motion with your tongue alternated with a circular motion around the base of the clitoris. Lightly suck on it, then use your tongue again.

Move down to the lips of the vagina and the perineum. Licking this area can cause great excitement; alternate it with pushing your tongue a little way inside the vagina. You can then move back to the clitoris and stimulate it again.

If you feel your partner is about to climax you can either progress or hold her back and build her up again. It depends what you both want at the time. If she is ready to climax, it is worth remembering that what most women want at that point are steady, rhythmic strokes at the same pressure. Many women complain that, just as they are about to orgasm, the

man changes the stroke or the pressure, or moves his tongue to another area, and so they lose the orgasm. For some women, it can be hard to get back to that point of climax without a lot more cunnilingus, so when they say 'keep doing that' they mean what you are doing right then. It is most pleasurable if you maintain a steady rhythm through her orgasm and press down a little more forcibly on the clitoris at that moment to relieve the sometimes painful sensitivity women feel there just after climaxing.

Linger awhile to kiss her post-orgasmic vulva and show your appreciation by kissing her mouth. That way she can smell and taste her own juices and have confidence that she tastes good.

'Place your darling on a couch, set her feet to your shoulders, clasp her waist, suck hard and let your tongue stir her overflowing love-temple: this is called Bahuchushita *(Sucked Hard).'*
Kama Sutra

Fellatio

The *Kama Sutra* lists eight ways of giving 'mouth congress'. They should be performed in sequence:

1. NOMINAL CONGRESS – hold the man's penis, place it in your mouth and move it between your lips.
2. BITING THE SIDES – hold the head of the penis and lightly press your lips and teeth along the length of the shaft.
3. PRESSING OUTSIDE – kiss the tip of the penis with closed lips.
4. PRESSING INSIDE – push only the head of the penis into your mouth and press with your lips.
5. KISSING – hold the penis in your hand and kiss it as if you were kissing your lover's lower lip.
6. RUBBING – stroke the entire shaft and head with your tongue.
7. SUCKING A MANGO FRUIT – place the penis halfway into your mouth and kiss and suck vigorously.
8. SWALLOWING IT UP – take the entire penis into your mouth and sucked as if swallowing it.

Most men adore being sucked and, as with women, they all vary in their needs. Some like it fast and hard as they approach climax, while others like a slower, steadier approach. Some only want the woman to take the head of the penis in her mouth while she strokes the shaft up and down with her hand. The only way to know is to ask.

BEGIN WITH GENTLE TEASING

Begin with light strokes of the tongue. Tease him before you take his penis in your mouth. Kiss his inner thighs and lightly use your tongue on his scrotum and the perineum behind it. You will be able to feel the testicles through the scrotum; hold them one at a time in your mouth, but be very gentle. Now work on the shaft, kissing and licking it, taking it in your mouth sideways. Once you have worked up the shaft, hold the penis in your hand firmly and start sucking and licking the sensitive head or glans and the ridge around the head. The underside of the penis is particularly sensitive, so keep bringing your tongue around to that spot. Start up a steady rhythm, using your hands and mouth together. Occasionally stop and make eye contact with him. It is exciting for a man to know you are enjoying yourself.

ENJOY THE CLIMAX

Bringing your partner to climax is easy if you know what he likes. The big question for some women is 'To swallow or not to swallow?' If you don't like it, don't do it, and tell him so beforehand in a considerate way. Letting him ejaculate over your breasts or stomach can be just as big a turn-on as ejaculating in your mouth.

Finish gently. Hold the penis in your mouth until he has finished ejaculating, then remove it slowly and kiss the shaft and testicles. Show your appreciation for the moment you have shared.

Sixty-nine

'If the pair of you lie side by side, facing opposite ways, and kiss each other's secret parts using the fifteen techniques described, it is known as Kakila (The Crow).' Kama Sutra

'Sixty-nine' is the common name for mutual oral sex. The term derives from the fact that six looks like an upside-down nine, and vice versa. There are two main ways you can arrange yourselves in this position. The first is for one of you to lie on your back with your partner kneeling over you, their genitals over your face, their mouth over your genitals. Or you may find it more comfortable to lie on your sides, with the man's head resting between the woman's thighs. Pillows placed between your knees may help to hold your legs apart and take pressure off your leg muscles.

CIRCLE OF ENERGY

You are creating a complete circle of energy in this position, which from a Taoist and Tantric perspective allows the Yin and Yang, or the Shiva and Shakti, energies to be exchanged at the same time.

Using this technique is more likely to lead to simultaneous orgasm once you are familiar with your partner's pace at reaching climax. It is also extremely arousing to be pleasuring each other in unison. However, as with everything else, it isn't for everyone.

DEEP

Deep penetration is one of the most desired sexual pleasures. The reasons for this are a mixture of biology and emotion. Regarding biology, depth strengthens the odds of conception. Emotionally, it appeals to our desire to be 'one' with the other person. Physically, it is just one of the entire repertoire of sensations, but should not be viewed as the ultimate one. No love-making session would be completely pleasurable if only deep penetration was experienced.
As it says in the *Tao*, *'Thrusting too shallowly the couple may not feel the greatest pleasure, too deeply and they may be injured.'* Variety is the key to maximum pleasure.

The positions in this section offer the potential to experience deep penetration completely, when that is what you desire, while the thrusting techniques provide the means of varying the sensations for both lovers.

Rhythm and Thrust

Whatever the sexual position, but especially with deep ones, the Eastern texts all suggest that the man uses what might be called 'systems' of thrusting and movement so that the woman achieves maximum pleasure. It appears to be assumed that the man will be pleasured, but that his reputation as a lover, and his ability to hold onto a woman, depends on his artful use of thrusting (Sets of Nine) and close observation of the woman.

SYSTEMS OF THRUST

The Sets of Nine are given in the *Kama Sutra* with instructions that the man should aim to go through as many sets as possible without ejaculating. They may also be used by the woman on the man when she is in a position that allows her control of movement.

The Taoists had a very similar system. Without practising some of the Taoist semen retention techniques, however, it is unlikely that many men will deliver the *'thousand loving thrusts'* that the Taoists recommended for any love-making session. They were numerologists and attributed the number nine with powerful Yang energy. Their method is based on nine shallow thrusts and one deep thrust.

For the nine shallow thrusts the man only allows the head of his penis to enter the woman, thus exciting and tantalizing her, while the deep thrust makes her feel satisfied. It is important that at no point should the man withdraw his penis completely. Physiologically, the shallow thrusts create a vacuum in the vagina and the deep thrust forces the air out, all of which adds to the woman's pleasure. Unlike the Sets of Nine, the number of shallow and deep thrusts remains constant, which may be easier to remember in the heat of the moment.

THE NINE MOVEMENTS OF MAN

The *Kama Sutra* also lists the Nine Movements of Man, to be used during intercourse. These are essentially ways of moving the penis that can be used in conjunction with the Sets of Nine or the Taoist method.

1. MOVING FORWARD – when the organs are brought together properly and directly.
2. CHURNING – when the penis is held with the hand and turned around in the vulva.
3. PIERCING – when the vagina is lowered and the upper part of it struck with the penis.
4. RUBBING – when the same thing is done on the lower part of the vagina.
5. PRESSING – when the vagina is pressed by the penis for a long time.

SETS OF NINE

1. Nine shallow, one deep
2. Eight shallow, two deep
3. Seven shallow, three deep
4. Six shallow, four deep
5. Five shallow, five deep
6. Four shallow, six deep
7. Three shallow, seven deep
8. Two shallow, eight deep
9. One shallow, eight deep

6. GIVING A BLOW – when the penis is removed some distance from the vagina, and then forcibly strikes it.

7. BLOW OF A BOAR – when only part of the vagina is rubbed by the penis.

8. BLOW OF A BULL – when both sides of the vagina are rubbed by the penis.

9. SPORTING OF A SPARROW – when the penis is moved up and down frequently, and without being taken out.

While the names of these movements are a lot more colourful than the actions they describe, it is undoubtedly true that women find it pleasurable to have their genitals rubbed in a variety of ways with the penis, and a number of men seem to be unaware of this. The effect of having the penis close to entry, but not inside, is highly exciting to women.

The Plough, The Flying White Tiger and Coition From Behind

Men are extremely aroused by rear-entry positions because they allow for deep penetration and more control over thrusting, and because they are stimulated by this view of a woman. For the woman, it is a comfortable position that allows good stimulation of the G-spot. As with woman-on-top positions, it allows freedom of hip movement. Also, the man, or the woman herself, can play with her clitoris, giving her a better chance of orgasm.

Another benefit is that it is physically less tiring for both the man and the woman. The woman may be supported by cushions, pillows and other bedding to take the strain off her arms and spine, while the man's body is relatively free to move as he likes without strain to any part of his body. If you are going to try these positions on a bed, make sure it is soft but firm.

THE PLOUGH

To achieve this position, taken from the *Kama Sutra*, the man kneels first while the woman sits astride his lap facing away from him. In this posture he can kiss her neck and shoulders while stroking her breasts. The woman then bends forward in a prayer-like prostration until he is able to enter her. Finally she stretches one leg back alongside his, while keeping the other leg bent, and rests her arms and head on pillows. The man thrusts into her while she uses her internal muscles to rhythmically stroke his penis.

THE FLYING WHITE TIGER

This Taoist alternative to The Plough is perhaps simpler in that the woman can assume a kneeling position that suits her while the man watches. She can tantalize him with her body as she finds the perfect arrangement of cushions to support her upper body while her forehead rests on the bed. The number of cushions she places beneath her belly and hips will determine the depth of penetration. The man should now enter her and hold her waist, pulling her slightly towards him.

The woman may remove cushions, or even add them, when she wants to alter the sensations she feels from her partner's penis. She may not be able to stimulate her clitoris like this manually, but rubbing against the cushions as her partner thrusts may be sufficient to help her achieve orgasm.

COITION FROM BEHIND

This is a variation from *The Perfumed Garden*, which explains that the attraction of the rear-entry position is that the man gets a full view of the vulva. It then goes on to describes a number of variations on this posture which are aimed at making the vulva protrude more. In this one the woman kneels and, when the man has entered her, she slips her arms around his elbows instead of placing them in front of her on the bed.

The Elephant Posture and Dark Cicada Clings to a Branch

These two postures allow the woman to lie on her belly while still achieving the desired deep penetration. Movement in these two positions can be gentle or strong, but both offer the possibility of rest during intercourse while allowing the man to move enough to maintain his erection, building up to orgasm at a pace that suits both partners.

THE ELEPHANT POSTURE

If you have started off in The Plough position (see page 72) and the woman feels strained, you can move into this position from the *Kama Sutra* without the man having to withdraw. If moving into this position, to prevent the man from 'slipping out', he should place a small cushion under the woman's pelvis as she drops down from the kneeling position because this will maintain his angle of entry. The woman may also want a cushion or pillow on which to rest her arms and head. The man supports himself with one hand on the bed, the other on her hip, so that his body is lying along hers but she is not taking any of his weight.

DARK CICADA CLINGS TO A BRANCH

In this position from *The Tao of Love*, the woman lies flat on her belly and spreads her legs as wide as is comfortable. Penetrating the woman, the man supports himself on his forearms, placing them level with her shoulders. This position is good if the woman has back pain. It allows deep penetration, but the cervix is protected by the position of the vagina. Also, it is a good one for G-spot stimulation.

The Swallow, Sampada-uttana-bandha and The Frog's Posture

Face-to-face postures also allow deep penetration. The classic Missionary Position is the most basic, although to achieve very deep penetration the woman's buttocks need to be raised. Face-to-face positions where the woman raises her legs and pelvis change the shape of the vagina, shortening it so that the penis is enclosed both tightly and deeply.

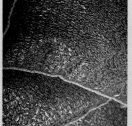

THE SWALLOW POSTURE

In this position from the *Kama Sutra*, the woman lies on her back and draws her knees up towards her chest, putting her feet in the air. The man kneels in front of her and penetrates her. The man remains still while the woman rotates her pelvis.

To give herself more support, and to take the weight off her leg muscles, the woman can rest her feet or legs on her partner's shoulders.

SAMPADA-UTTANA-BANDHA

In this alternative from the *Ananga Ranga*, the woman lies on her back and the man sits with a straight back facing her, his legs opened to either side of her body. He places her legs on his shoulders then penetrates her, pulling her hips toward him as necessary. This might be best done on the floor with the man using the side of a bed or other furniture to support his back.

THE FROG'S POSTURE

According to *The Perfumed Garden*, the man places the woman on her back and gently raises her thighs until her heels are almost touching her buttocks. The ease, or extent, to which this can be done depends on the woman's flexibility. He then penetrates her and holds her knees in place by placing them under his armpits.

If you are feeling particularly agile, the final move of this position entails the man pulling the woman's upper body towards him at the moment of ejaculation.

The Archimedean Screw and Purushayita

A favourite position for both sexes is when the woman is on top. Apart from the fact that it gives the man a rest, it also allows him to have a full view of the woman, which is a big turn-on for him. He can watch the movement of her breasts and he can see her facial expressions of pleasure. Also, it releases him from a position of control.

While many women love to be on top, some feel self-conscious about how exposed their bodies are in this position, and every little perceived imperfection inhibits them from trying it. If you feel like that, remember that men rarely think critically about a woman's body during sex.

THE ARCHIMEDEAN SCREW

From *The Perfumed Garden*, this is a simple woman-on-top position. The man lies on his back while the woman sits astride him and lowers herself onto his penis. She leans forward, supported by her arms and keeping her belly away from the man's. The woman moves either up and down or in a circular motion, changing rhythm and direction as she pleases, giving herself and the man a variety of sensations.

PURUSHAYITA

In this alternative from the *Ananga Ranga*, the woman squats over the man's thighs with her knees in front of her and her heels on the ground. After inserting the man's penis she squeezes her legs tightly together and rotates her waist as though spinning a hula hoop, changing direction when desired.

If you find it hard to stay balanced in a squatting position, you could hold your lover's hands, interlacing your fingers with palms facing, to keep you steady.

Swimming Fishes and The Camel's Hump

Unlike other rear-entry positions, which require the woman to be on her belly or facing downwards, these use an upright kneeling position helped by the use of furniture, such as the edge of a bed or a sofa, to support the woman's weight. The man also needs to support less of his own weight, meaning that, for both, the positions can be sustained for longer. In these positions, the man is in control of pace and depth, so the woman will have to communicate her needs to him.

SWIMMING FISHES

For this *Kama Sutra* position you will need a sofa or bed for the woman to support herself on, and the man will need a cushion on the floor to support his knee.

The man places his left knee on the cushion, keeping his other knee raised, his thigh parallel to the floor. The woman sits on his right knee, facing away from him, keeping her right knee facing forwards and her left knee pointing towards the floor. With the man holding her around her waist, the woman drops her body forwards,

supporting her weight on the bed or sofa. Now, the man stands up and, as he does so, slides his hands down both of the woman's thighs and lifts her into a position where he can penetrate her. The woman bends her legs behind his back as he thrusts into her.

This sounds more difficult than it is. If the woman is well supported, she shouldn't feel any strain. If you start to feel uncomfortable change to a position in which you feel more relaxed.

THE CAMEL'S HUMP

Don't let the name put you off. This posture from *The Perfumed Garden* is an excellent one for supple women. Those who are not so supple could adapt the position to suit, using furniture to support them. The position gives the man a very exciting view of the woman's genitals, and he can clearly watch his own thrusting movements.

The woman stands and bends forwards until she touches her toes. The man, standing behind her, penetrates her, clasping her upper thighs to him. The man then controls the depth and pace of thrusting.

A Pair of Flying Ducks and
The Mutual View of the Buttocks

Another version of the woman-on-top position has the woman facing away from the man. This is a solution for women who feel inhibited sitting astride a man. By facing away, they have private space to experience the sensations and to play with their own body while enjoying penetration. This also benefits the man, who can watch his lover moving on his erection while being able to enjoy his own sensations without having to maintain eye contact with the woman.

A PAIR OF FLYING DUCKS

This is a variation on the basic Taoist position. The man lies supine, his legs straight, while the woman sits astride him facing his feet. It is more comfortable if the woman adopts a kneeling posture, as her legs can then support her weight. A squatting posture would mean the man taking her weight on his pelvis, which may be fine if the woman is very light.

The woman puts his penis inside her. She can stroke her clitoris and her breasts and the man can play with her buttocks and back. Doing this in front of a mirror would add an exciting dimension, especially for the woman.

THE MUTUAL VIEW OF THE BUTTOCKS

From *The Perfumed Garden*, this is a more athletic version of A Pair of Flying Ducks.
The woman sits astride the man's penis, facing his feet and with her legs in front of
her. The man raises his legs, clasping the sides of her body with them as she leans
over to touch the floor. Supported by her hands, she is able to control her
movements. At the same time, she has a view of his buttocks, and he of hers.

Cat and Mice Share a Hole

This Taoist deep-penetration position is again a woman-on-top one, this time with the woman facing the man. It is a relaxing position, and one that a couple might find useful if they have become tired through active thrusting and neither has had an orgasm. It is a good choice for a woman to get plenty of clitoral stimulation.

CAT AND MICE SHARE A HOLE

The man lies on his back, his legs straight and relaxed. The woman sits astride him and helps him to penetrate her. She then lowers her entire body onto his, her legs lying on top of his.

Pleasure doesn't come from active thrusting, but through subtle movements of both partners, such as side-to-side rolls, or the woman can hold the man's shoulders and gently move up and down. The woman can control her clitoral stimulation doing this, and by using her vaginal muscles she can heighten the man's sensation at the same time.

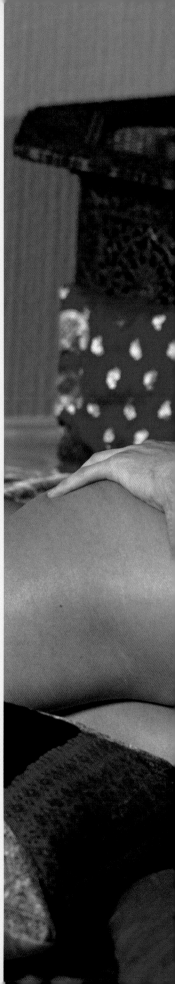

Padmini Posture and Splitting the Bamboo

These women-supine positions are ideal for using in sequence. They both allow deep penetration without causing strain to either partner.

PADMINI POSTURE

In this position from the *Ananga Ranga* the woman lies on her back and raises her knees to her chest. The man kneels in front of her, his knees on either side of her hips, and from this position he enters her.

The woman's vagina is narrowed and there is tension in the muscles, which adds to the sensation of sexual arousal that she feels. Similarly, the man's pleasure is heightened by the tightness of the vagina around his penis.

SPLITTING THE BAMBOO

From Padmini, you could move to this posture from the *Kama Sutra.* The woman lies on her back and places one foot on the man's shoulder. The man kneels in front of her with his knees on either side of her hips. He enters her and she stretches her other leg out placing it over his other shoulder. The woman alternates the position of her legs so that she 'dances' to a rhythm of pleasure while the man remains static.

Silkworm and Water Crane

These Taoist positions are considered to be healing sexual positions in that the depth of thrust can affect the health of internal organs in a similar way to Shiatsu massage. These two could also be used in sequence, as the second position offers relaxation after the first. In both these positions it is the woman's movement that keeps the man stimulated and erect.

SILKWORM

This position is considered helpful for increasing energy in both lovers.

The woman lies supine and the man lies on top as in the Missionary Position and penetrates her deeply. The woman then rotates her pelvis in both directions alternately, which may lead her to orgasm.

WATER CRANE

This is helpful for the reproductive organs, the stomach and the spleen.

The woman lies supine with her lower back supported by pillows and her legs wrapped around her partner's waist. The man supports himself on his hands and knees, his back straight and parallel to the floor. He then penetrates her and remains still while she rotates her pelvis in both directions alternately.

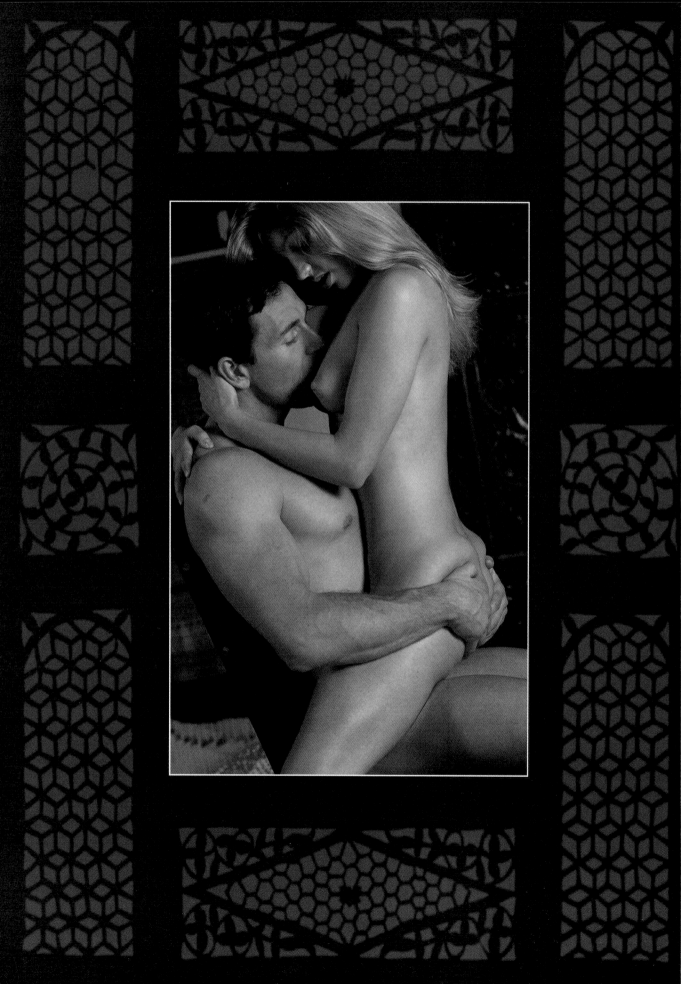

GENTLE

Not all sexual intercourse has to be fast and furious. There are times when you may want physical intimacy, and a bit more than cuddling and stroking, but neither of you wants energetic sex. Also, with some disabilities, or if the woman is pregnant, many positions, if not impossible, will be uncomfortable.

Gentle sex is not sex lacking in desire. It may not be the type of sex you want in the first flush of lust, but it is an essential element of the sex repertoire of lovers who want to know each other in a more sensual and complete way. There are times when we need to take time for sex, or when we need to resolve sexual problems. Taking sex gently is the way.

Soft-entry Sex and Side Positions

Gentle sex can also be soft-style sex. Soft-style is penetrative sex when the man cannot get an erection. This is a common state and does not reflect on a man's sexual ability. The state is well documented in terms of both medical and psychological conditions, and it is often the result of a complex set of factors that can affect a man at any time, regardless of age.

The most basic technique for soft-style sex requires some practice, a little lubricant and a gentle touch. Either partner puts some lubricant around the vaginal entrance, opening it with their fingers at the same time. The man puts the head of his penis in the vagina, then, using his forefinger and thumb, makes a tight ring around the base of his penis. This pressure helps the blood to stay in the head of the penis. The man can thrust gently and the woman can help him by using her vaginal

muscles to stroke and stimulate his penis. Very often this will give a man a full erection. Women also like the feeling of a man growing hard inside them; in many ways this is more erotic than an erection achieved normally.

Side-by-side positions are the best ones for soft-style sex, although they are not exclusively for it. Some are face to face while others have the man enfolding the woman from behind. Penetration is not so deep in this position anyway, which makes intercourse more comfortable for women if their partner has a large penis. They also enjoy the feeling of being 'surrounded' by the man's body, as in the classic Spoons position (see page 107), when each can quietly become aware of the other's body, letting desire arise slowly. The woman can

rub her buttocks softly against the man's genitals to arouse him. In turn, the man can stroke the woman's breasts, hips and buttocks as well as play with her clitoris, bringing her to orgasm manually. If he has an erection, in this position the man can also thrust for longer without ejaculating. It is ideal, therefore, for a long, relaxing session with the added benefit that it is a comfortable position in which to fall asleep.

On some occasions time and a little tenderness are all that are required to arouse desire where there was none before. No person's libido operates at full capacity all the time, and anyway it isn't necessary that it should be so. In its own way laid-back sex is as fulfilling and sensual as the more raunchy stuff.

Yab Yum and Upavishta

These positions can be used with or without penetration, or to help the man get an erection. The basic position – Yab Yum as described in the *Kama Sutra* and Upavishta from the *Ananga Ranga* – can also be subtly varied so that both partners experience a range of genital sensations.

YAB YUM

For this face-to-face posture, the man may want something to support his back. Also, make sure he is sitting on something soft and comfortable.

The man sits with his legs crossed and the woman sits astride him, her arms and legs round his back. The position can be used to arouse both partners by first gently rubbing against each others genitals before attempting penetration. Obviously, if the man is erect, he can penetrate the woman immediately.

If you are using this position with penetration, the woman can make circular or sideways movements with her hips to keep herself and the man stimulated. It is a good position for becoming aware and using the senses meditatively.

UPAVISHTA

The Upavishta is the same basic position as Yab Yum. The *Ananga Ranga* sub-divides it into ten variations, and Upapad-asana and Sanyaman-asana are two of these.

Sanyaman-asana

Again in a sitting posture, the man hooks his arms under the woman's legs, cradling them in his elbows, holding her back with his hands. Here, lifting the woman's legs will alter the sensation by shortening the vagina.

Upapad-asana

When in a sitting posture, the woman slightly raises one leg by placing her hand under her thigh and lifting it. She holds onto the man by placing her other arm around his neck.

Like this, it will be more difficult for the woman to move, so the man could try rolling his hips from side to side. Basically, as with all these positions, try it and see what is best for you.

Yawning Posture and Nagara-bandha

These two positions from the *Kama Sutra* and *Ananga Ranga* respectively are very similar. You can use each one on its own or move from one into the other, with the woman staying in the same position throughout. Both these postures are said to be good for women who have problems with moving their hips while lying on their back. However, this doesn't mean that the woman has to be completely passive. The man is in control of thrusting, but she can still play an equal part by simply moving her legs into different positions.

YAWNING POSTURE

For this position from the *Kama Sutra,* the woman lies supine and spreads her legs to either side of the man's waist, keeping them in a V-shape with toes pointed. He kneels close to her, his knees to either side of her hips, so that his thighs support hers. He supports his weight on his arms, but does not lean over her too much.

By changing the position of one or both of her legs (which she will probably want to do in any case because of muscle tension), either by bending, lifting or dropping them down, the woman can control both her genital sensations and those of her partner.

NAGARA-BANDHA

From the Yawning Posture the man could move into this position from the *Ananga Ranga*, or you can use it independently. It may be possible for him to adopt it without withdrawing his penis, but if that doesn't work, the woman could hold and rub his penis for him while he moves his legs, as a loving way of keeping the connection with him, and also helping him to keep his erection. Everyone loves to be wanted, and men adore their penis to be desired and admired. Little gestures, like keeping hold of his penis, which tells him you want more, will mean a lot to him.

With the woman lying on her back, the man opens the woman's legs and sits between them, spreading his own legs out to either side of her. He rests her legs over his and holds them around his waist.

In this position the man can enjoy an open view of the woman's genitals and of his penis entering them. This is exciting in itself and the woman could lie back and let him experiment with his movements to see what effect they have. It is not always necessary for both partners to be active at the same time.

Yin Yang Posture and Shakti

These postures are both wonderful for sustaining penetration while taking a break, particularly in the middle of an energetic session. Also, by facing each other and maintaining eye contact while resting, there is a subtle signal that the session is not over but may be resumed.

YIN YANG POSTURE

In this Taoist posture, the man lies on his side resting his head on his hand, his legs straight but relaxed and crossed at the ankles. The woman lies on her back at right angles to him, with her legs draped over his hips.

After the man has penetrated her in this position, both of them stay still. The woman can still use her vaginal muscles to massage the penis in this position, keeping it hard. But the main aim of the pose is rest.

SHAKTI

This is a much simplified version of a Tantric posture that is best performed by yoga experts or gymnasts.

In this version, the man sits with his back straight and his legs stretched out in front. He could use the sofa or the edge of the bed for this. The woman sits sideways on his lap, her right arm around his shoulder. The man penetrates her. Then the woman keeps her legs together and bends them so her feet are pointing behind the man. They can then sit quietly kissing, talking and holding each other.

If the woman feels supple enough to take this position a step further, she can lean back, supporting her body by placing a hand on his leg, then swing her right leg over his head to rest it on his left shoulder. The results if you are not supple are easily imagined, and are to be avoided unless you both have a good sense of humour.

The Swing and A Singing Monkey Holding a Tree

Excellent for prolonged love making, these positions can be alternately energetic and restful. By contrast with the previous sitting postures, these both require specific simple movements, but as with all the sex positions, you can experiment and add your own subtle variations.

THE SWING

The man and woman face each other in this position from the *Kama Sutra*, and after penetration embrace closely, their legs bent around each other's backs. They then use the weight of their bodies to create a back-and-forth motion, just like a playground swing.

The movement doesn't have to be dramatic. Alternate strong movements with more gentle ones and you will last longer.

A SINGING MONKEY HOLDING A TREE

In this Taoist position the woman is the singing monkey. A straight-backed dining chair with a cushion on it is an ideal prop.

The man sits on the chair while the woman straddles his lap, facing him and holding onto him with both hands. She helps him to penetrate her, and he then places his hands under her buttocks. He can then help her bounce her bottom up and down. Again, the movement can be alternated between strong and gentle.

It will help the woman to have more control if the chair has struts along the bottom on which she can balance her feet. The woman can also try other movements. For example, she could lock her fingers around his neck and, leaning back, use an in-and-out or circular motion. If you want to turn on the man even more, do this in front of a mirror.

The Fusion of Love, Drawing the Bow and Jrimbhita-asana

Side positions are relaxing, intimate and also instill a feeling of balance between partners – neither one is in a superior position. As stated earlier, side positions are ideal for soft-style sex, but some are better than others.

THE FUSION OF LOVE

In this beautifully named, simple posture from *The Perfumed Garden*, the woman lies on her right side and the man on his left, facing her. The man keeps his lower leg straight and raises his other leg, placing it over the woman's hips. He then pulls the woman's upper leg towards the leg he has placed over her hips, and penetrates her.

DRAWING THE BOW

Also from *The Perfumed Garden*, in this posture the man lies behind the woman, placing both his legs between hers. He then penetrates her and holds her to him by her shoulders.

The woman then pulls the man's feet up towards her and holds them, thus creating a bow-and-arrow shape. This position is not as suitable for soft-style sex, but it is a useful variation of the side position that is much less strenuous, and more comfortable, than it sounds.

JRIMBHITA-ASANA

This rear-entry alternative to Drawing the Bow, from the *Ananga Ranga*, simply has the man place pillows and cushions under the woman's head and hips, raising her hips until he can kneel and enter her. In this way, the woman's body is curved like a bow.

Although this could be a deep-penetration posture, it can also be used as a more meditative pose with the woman resting on her belly and the man kneeling, using only gentle thrusts.

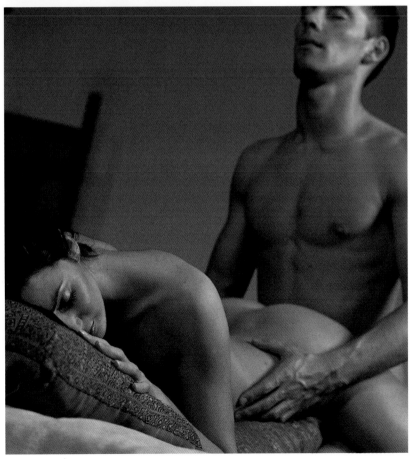

Eternal Bliss and Lotus

Both of these positions from the *Kama Sutra* are relaxing and are ideal when you desire languorous sex during which you can talk to each other while still enjoying the sensation of penetration.

ETERNAL BLISS

Based on the image of a woman waiting for her lover to return to her after a long separation, this position is seductive and tender. It could be a good position to use when making up after a disagreement.

The woman sits on the floor in a kind of mermaid pose, her legs together, her head turned away from her lower body looking over her shoulder.

The man kneels at her feet and strokes them. As he does this the woman half-turns towards him. Seeing this as an invitation, the man moves his body up hers, stroking her and kissing her body until he is able to embrace her shoulders and kiss her mouth.

The woman then rolls over more onto to her side to allow him to enter her from behind. Having done this, the man then curls his body around hers.

LOTUS

This pose allows a couple to relax after a vigorous session of sex, and can even be a position to fall asleep in, albeit a slightly unconventional one.

The man sits on the bed with his left leg stretched out in front and his right foot flat on the bed, knee raised. He places his hands behind him to support himself. The woman sits diagonally across his lap, her left leg under his right. She too leans back on her two hands for support. In this position he enters her, and they hold onto each other's right shoulder.

Holding on to each other with one hand while still leaning on one elbow, they each lower themselves onto the bed. The woman now extends her legs on either side of her partner's body.

As they both lie supine, their heads at opposite ends of the bed, the man can touch the woman's legs. They are still together, but at the same time lying apart.

Maharajah and Spoons

The Maharajah position, from the *Kama Sutra,* will make the man feel like a king, pampered and in receipt of loving devotion, while he relaxes completely. Afterwards you can move into the most relaxing position of all, Spoons, pose in which you may become aroused again to continue love making.

MAHARAJAH

This gentle position from the *Kama Sutra* puts the woman in control and allows the man to be completely relaxed and feel that he is receiving a lot of loving attention. Use cushions or pillows to support the man's back so that he is completely comfortable.

The woman sits upright with her knees pointing outwards and the soles of her feet touching. The man sits inside her legs, placing his legs over hers and wrapping them around her back. In this position they can embrace and kiss.

The man then puts his arms behind his back and lowers himself back onto the cushions. He then lifts first one leg then the other, placing his ankles over the woman's shoulders, while she holds his legs. They can then either remain still, with the woman using her pelvic muscles to squeeze his penis, or she can gently bounce up and down to stimulate them both.

SPOONS

This is a universally loved position, mentioned in all the texts. The man lies behind the woman, cupping her body with his. This is the gentlest way to end any love-making session, or to arouse the desire to start another just by using Tantric awareness. While lying in this position, become aware of your partner's breathing and match your breathing to theirs; at the same time both pay attention to the sensations of warmth and energy at the points where your bodies touch.

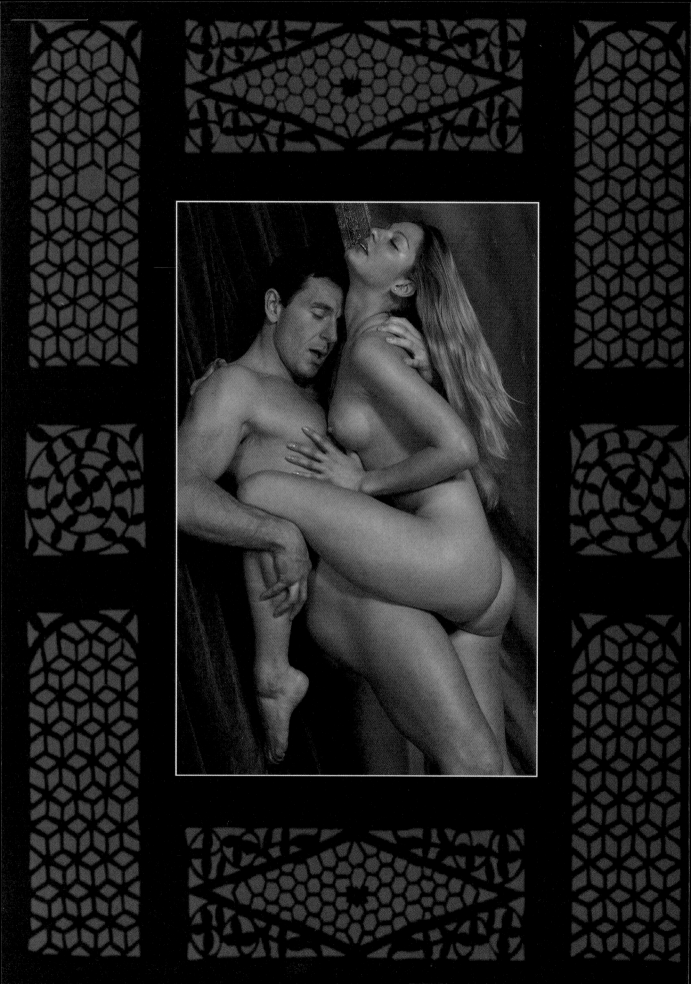

FAST

The *Kama Sutra* says:
*'Passionate actions and amorous gesticulations or movements which arise
on the spur of the moment, and during sexual intercourse, cannot
be defined and are as irregular as dreams.'*
It goes on to compare this sexual passion with the way a horse at full speed will
gallop on regardless of obstacles in its way:
*'In the same manner a loving pair become blind with passion
in the heat of congress, and go on with great impetuosity paying
not the least regard to excess.'*

The Instant Fulfilment of Desire

The intense desire for sex can arise at any time. It needn't be confined to the early days of attraction, although that is when you are both most likely to feel it. It demands immediate satisfaction, usually without requiring any foreplay, as the arousal is already intense without any need to charm it out.

When leading busy lives our sensitivity to this desire can easily be lost. Many of us have been increasingly losing touch with our natural rhythms and we sometimes tend to ignore the messages our bodies send us.

Becoming more sensitive to the messages your body is sending you will help you stay more attuned to all your desires, including your sexual ones. In other words, if your body tells you that you need to eat, then eat, and if you feel like sex, don't wait until Friday night because that's the night you usually set aside for sex. Use your imagination to find a way to satisfy the desire at the time it arises. You may feel this is impossible, but there are usually ways. Use the telephone, or email. Tell your partner that you want them. Convey to them the urgency of your desire.

This will arouse them before they even see you. Use your body language and 'private' words to communicate you still want sex as soon as possible. If your time is your own, then try surprising each other. Women: leave your clothes and underwear lying in the hallway where he can follow it like a trail. Men: arrive with an erection and have sex without waiting to get to a bedroom.

FAST SEX

There is always a place for fast sex in long-term relationships. However long we have been with a partner we will always experience moments of heightened desire. These can arise by themselves, or may be prompted by a memory, or a book you are reading, a film, or the sight of other lovers. It is important to act on this craving for urgent fulfilment when we feel it. Expressing a sudden yearning is a way of refreshing ourselves and so renewing our sexual relationship.

Giving way to impulses is not necessarily indulgent, it is healthy, whereas checking our impulses because they seem in appropriate can be very unhealthy for our emotions and for our relationships.

Act on your desire for fast sex as often as you can, using your imagination to sustain your lust and arouse that of your partner.

FROM THE EAST

The Eastern texts have much to say about reading the signs of passion and arousal in your partner (see page 44). They realized that passion could arise quickly, and that it should be satisfied quickly, although it seems that this is out of fear of losing a partner to another lover. They have left us a repertoire of sexual positions that lend themselves wonderfully well to instant gratification.

Congress of a Cow, Late Spring Donkey and Dhanuka–vyanta–bandha

It is noticeable that various positions are common to all the ancient texts. Sometimes there are slight variations while at other times they are identical. Congress of a Cow from the *Kama Sutra* and Late Spring Donkey from the *Tao* are examples of identical positions, while Dhanuka-vyanta-bandha is an easier variation from the *Ananga Ranga*. Whichever name you prefer, this position is ideal for fast sex as it is unnecessary for either partner to undress completely. All that needs to be exposed are the genitals.

CONGRESS OF A COW AND LATE SPRING DONKEY

The woman bends forward touching the floor, supporting herself with her hands. If bending that far over makes you feel strained, support yourself on a desk, chair, side of the bath, or whatever is closest to hand.

The man enters her from behind, clasping her round the waist. As the woman is supported, she can join in the thrusting action with the man.

DHANUKA-VYANTA-BANDHA

This alternative posture from the *Ananga Ranga* also translates as The Cow Posture. Instead of bending over, the woman drops down onto all fours and, as the text says, *'The husband, approaching from behind, falls upon her waist, and enjoys her as if he were a bull.'*

Again, this can be enjoyed in an instant. Plus, the woman, if she remains partially clothed, is likely to excite the man more with the view of her buttocks.

Driving the Peg and The Three Footprints

Standing postures are as popular in the contemporary erotic imagination as they obviously were long ago, and are synonymous with the instant gratification of desire. However, positions in which the woman is lifted up often need some form of support in order for the couple to hold them comfortably. Walls, anywhere, are well-tried forms of support. Try these positions in the hallway, which is a very erotic venue as it suggests you could barely even wait for your lover to get in the house.

DRIVING THE PEG

The name suggests pace and intensity, although *The Perfumed Garden* does caution against damaging the penis. It is referring to the possibility of the couple collapsing from the strain of sustaining this position.

The man leans his upper back against a wall to support himself. The woman throws her arms around the man's neck, and raises her legs and clasps them around his waist, resting her feet against the wall. This gives her support and some leverage to thrust against the man. *The Perfumed Garden* says, *'The man now introduces his member, and the woman is then as if hanging on a peg'*. Supporting her buttocks, the man can then help the woman to move with him, or they can take it in turns to make thrusting movements.

THE THREE FOOTPRINTS

This is a variation from the *Kama Sutra* and, as the name implies, three feet are kept on the ground. For many people this is an easier position to maintain than Driving the Peg.

The man stands with both feet on the ground while the woman lifts one of her legs. Depending on the height difference between the partners, the woman can either wrap her leg around his waist or round the back of his thigh. Either way the man supports her by placing a hand under her buttocks.

If there is a big height difference between the man and woman, it may be impossible for the woman to keep one foot on the ground, in which case using the first two steps of a staircase might resolve the problem.

Shiva's Dance

This Tantric position is another that can be adopted quickly when the urge takes you. It is a variation on the standing poses that are so popular for fast sex, perhaps because the conjure images of sex in illicit or unusual places, and because they provide intense physical sensations.

This Tantric position can be adopted quickly, but can also include stillness and gentleness. Being still during penetration allows build-up of genital sensation and sexual tension. In practising stillness you become more aware of your body's natural flow, and you will also become highly attuned to your partner's rhythms.

It is easier to get into this standing pose if the woman starts in a sitting position.

With the woman sitting with her legs apart, the man squats between her legs and she wraps her legs round his back. The man lifts the woman up onto his penis while she clasps his neck and grasps his waist with her thighs. The woman then thrusts vigorously against the man, who is able to support her buttocks with his hands, while helping her movements at the same time.

If the woman feels tired, the man can lower her into a standing position, possibly supported by furniture, so that both can rest but he can remain inside her. They can then become aware of the build-up of feelings until the urge to thrust hard is felt again. At this point the man picks up his partner, still penetrating her, but this time he lays her down and they resume vigorous thrusting. It may not always be possible for the man to stay inside his partner while changing position. As always it is the spirit of the position that is important, rather than following it slavishly.

Turning Dragon, Puja and Namaste

This posture is mentioned in all the Eastern texts, each with slight variations. Here we have three positions, the first two fairly similar and the last providing a grand finale.

TURNING DRAGON

The woman lies on her back in this Taoist posture, while the man kneels in front of her and, using one hand, pushes her feet up past her breasts. He holds his penis with the other hand and guides it into her. The man holds the woman's feet throughout, and it is the man who controls movement.

This position shortens and tightens the vagina.

PUJA

In this Tantric variation, the man places his knees on either side of the woman's hips. He folds her knees back to her chest, and she supports herself by placing her feet on his chest.

He holds her knees together, crossing his arms over the top of them. This helps him to thrust more energetically and, by holding her knees together, her vagina can grip him more tightly.

NAMASTE

It would be possible, and pleasurable, to move into this posture, which is also Tantric, at the end of a lively session in Puja.

Immediately after orgasm, and with the woman gripping the penis as tightly as possible with her vagina, the man slides his legs out of a kneeling position into a sitting position, holding the woman's legs together as he does this. He then raises her feet to touch first his mouth, then nose, followed by eyes, finally touching them to the crown of his head. It is said that, in performing these movements, the man will have all his desires fulfilled.

This can also be used as a thrusting position, but there is something more pleasing about using it as a closing position in which the 'still' qualities of Tantra can be experienced.

Veshtita Asana and A Phoenix Plays on a Red Cave

Both of these positions, the first from the *Ananga Ranga*, the second Taoist, are suitable to be used in the sequence they are shown. These positions are good for providing the strong sensations desired in fast sex and for allowing deep penetration at the same time.

VESHTITA ASANA

The *Ananga Ranga* says that this position is perfect for those burning with desire. As it says: *'The woman lies on her back cross-legged and raises her feet a little.'* There are two of ways of interpreting this:

1. The woman crosses her legs over her belly so that the vulva and buttocks are exposed and the man can enter her easily, kneeling in front of her.

2. To achieve a different sensation, the woman could lay her legs flat, her inner thighs facing upwards, crossing her legs loosely below the knees. The man would then adopt a Missionary Position to enter her. A cushion under the buttocks might make this more pleasurable for both.

A PHOENIX PLAYS ON A RED CAVE

This Taoist posture is for the flexible woman with strong leg muscles. It's one that is sure to get any man going. And if he is already excited, it will increase his ardour.

The woman lies on her back and holds her legs in the air. To make this more exciting, she could hold them wide apart so the man has a full view of her genitals. He can then penetrate her from a kneeling or Missionary Position, slipping his arms through and under hers, placing them on the floor either side of her waist to support himself. The woman is not in a position to thrust, so this is another pose where the man has most control of movement. However, if both of you want a rest from thrusting action, the woman could roll her hips from side to side, which would give both partners a different sensation.

If neither partner is in a hurry for penetration, the man could give the woman some oral pleasure while she is offering herself to him in this way.

Wild Abandon and The Stallion

These energetic poses from the *Kama Sutra* require some strength and suppleness. Happily, in the heat of the moment you may find that you have more stamina than you think. You can always adapt the position to your own ability.

WILD ABANDON

The man sits upright with his legs straight out in front of him. The woman kneels astride his lap, her knees clasping his hips. They wrap their arms around each other's backs, at which point the man can enter her. With the man holding her waist and supporting her, the woman leans back, placing her palms on the floor. She then lifts her left leg over his right shoulder.

Now the man also leans back, supporting himself on his hands, and uses his arms to raise his buttocks off the floor. This also makes the woman lift herself with him, although she always keeps her right foot on the ground for support. They finish by raising both their bodies to clasp each other and, staying in this position, they rock their bodies as strongly as they wish.

THE STALLION

This pose requires the woman to have a flexible spine so it is advisable for those with back problems to either avoid it or take care to adapt it to their needs. Similarly, the man should take care not to thrust too deeply

The man kneels on the floor with his legs together, while the woman kneels by his left side facing behind him. She clasps his shoulders and he holds her waist.

Now she lunges her left leg over his thighs, the man always supporting her upper body. In this position the man can play with the woman's genitals.

The man now takes the woman's right hand from his shoulder and gently twists her round until she is facing away from him. He then lowers her onto pillows and, holding her by the hips, enters her from behind.

The Somersault and Hari-vikrama-utthita-bandha

The first position from *The Perfumed Garden,* is simple yet reflects the comic eroticism of the writer's imagination and his knowledge of what happens when lust arises quickly. The second, from the *Ananga Ranga,* is an ancient form of a well-known posture that was thought to be particularly pleasing to young women.

THE SOMERSAULT

The woman tantalizes the man by revealing parts of her body but not all of it. She then especially takes care to give him a glimpse of her buttocks, after which, she bends over to reveal them more fully. On seeing this, the man grabs her from behind and tips her over onto her back. He pushes her legs up onto her chest and leans against them to hold her steady so that he can enter her from a kneeling position.

HARI-VIKRAMA-UTTHITA-BANDHA

The man stands, supported either by a wall or something to keep him steady, and the woman faces him.

She places her arms around his neck and he lifts one of her legs and holds it steady. In this position he enters her and they move together.

Index

Page numbers in *italics* refer to illustrations.

PICTURE ACKNOWLEDGEMENTS IN SOURCE ORDER:

Special Photography: Darren Paul

Bridgeman Art Library, London/New York /Bonora 9, /Private Collection 12, 24
Christie's Images 19, 20
Corbis UK Ltd/Burstein Collection 14
The Art Archive/Victoria and Albert Museum, London/Sally Chappell 10
Octopus Publishing Group Limited/Darren Paul front cover, back cover, 2, 3, 5, 6, 11, 23, 26, 26-27, 28, 29, 30, 31, 32, 33, 34, 35, 36, 36-37, 38, 39, 40, 41 top, 41 bottom, 42, 43, 44, 45, 46, 46-47, 48, 49, 50, 51, 52, 53, 54 left, 54 right, 55 top, 55 bottom right, 56, 57, 58, 59, 60, 62, 63, 64, 65, 66, 67, 68, 70, 71, 72, 73, 74, 75 top, 75 bottom, 76 left, 76 right, 77 top right, 77 bottom left, 78, 79 top, 79 bottom left, 80 left, 80 right, 81, 81 right, 82 top right, 82 bottom left, 83 top, 83 bottom left, 84, 84-85, 86 left, 86 right, 87, 88, 89 top, 89 bottom right, 90, 92 top right, 92 bottom, 93, 94, 95 top, 95 bottom, 96, 97 top, 97 bottom left, 98, 99 top left, 99 top right, 99 bottom right, 100 left, 100 right, 101, 102, 103 top, 103 bottom, 104 left, 104 right, 105 top left, 105 top right, 105 bottom right, 106 left, 106 right, 107 top, 107 bottom, 108, 110, 111, 112 top right, 112 bottom left, 113, 114, 115, 116 left, 116 right, 117 left, 117 right, 118 left, 118 right, 119 top right, 119 bottom left, 120, 121 Top, 121 bottom left, 122 left, 122 right, 123 top left, 123 top right, 123 bottom right, 124 left, 124 right, 125 right, 125 top right
Werner Forman Archive/Private Collection 17, 22